LOAF TIN BAKES

LOAF TIN BAKES

Easy Cakes for Every Occasion

FLAVIE MILLET-JOANNON
PHOTOGRAPHS BY SANDRINE SAADI

First published in Great Britain in 2026
by Hamlyn, an imprint of
Octopus Publishing Group Ltd
Carmelite House
50 Victoria Embankment
London EC4Y 0DZ
www.octopusbooks.co.uk

An Hachette UK Company
www.hachette.co.uk

The authorized representative in the EEA
is Hachette Ireland, 8 Castlecourt Centre,
Dublin 15, D15 XTP3, Ireland (email: info@hbgi.ie)

Originally published in France as *Il Était un Cake*
by Hachette Pratique in 2021
Il Était un Cake copyright © Hachette Livre
(Hachette Pratique) 2021

Text by Flavie Millet-Joannon
Photographs by Sandrine Saadi

Translation copyright © Octopus Publishing
Group Ltd 2026

Distributed in the US by Hachette Book Group
1290 Avenue of the Americas, 4th and 5th Floors
New York, NY 10104

Distributed in Canada by Canadian Manda Group
664 Annette St., Toronto, Ontario, Canada M6S 2C8

All rights reserved. No part of this work may be
reproduced or utilized in any form or by any means,
electronic or mechanical, including photocopying,
recording or by any information storage and
retrieval system, without the prior written
permission of the publisher.

Flavie Millet-Joannon asserts the moral right to be
identified as the author of this work.

ISBN: 978-0-600-63962-6
eISBN: 978-0-600-63963-3

A CIP catalogue record for this book is available
from the British Library.

Printed and bound in China.

10 9 8 7 6 5 4 3 2 1

Staff credits for this edition:
Publisher: Kate Fox
Junior Commissioning Editor: Isabel Jessop
Assistant Editor: Alice Gawthrop
Art Director: Jaz Bahra
Editor: Rosie Hilton
Designer: Geoff Fennell
Copyeditor: Emily Preece-Morrison
Production Manager: Caroline Alberti

CONTENTS

INTRODUCTION	9
BEFORE YOU START	10
BASIC RECIPES	20
THE CLASSICS	30
VIVE LE CHOCOLAT!	46
MARBLED TO PERFECTION	66
BRILLIANTLY NUTTY	88
A TOUCH OF CITRUS	106
A TRIP TO THE MARKET	126
PÂTISSERIE FAVOURITES	142
OUTSIDE THE BOX	160
GLOSSARY	184
INDEX	186
ACKNOWLEDGEMENTS	192

INTRODUCTION

The idea for this book spent a long time developing in my head. I had already been thinking about it for several months before testing any recipes. I wanted to create a book of indulgent loaf cake recipes that were different, but most importantly very simple, so that they could be made by as many people as possible.

This 100 per cent loaf cakes book is partly about my desire to demonstrate that, with very little equipment (a loaf tin is generally one of the basic items lurking at the back of everyone's kitchen cupboard) and in very little time, you can produce a jolly nice cake that can be enjoyed as a dessert by all. Experienced bakers will also find several recipes that involve a little more technique, such as making ganache, creams, icings and also meringue.

I chose the loaf cake theme because I love these simple cakes and because there is something to please every palate and taste. Another reason was because loaf cakes are part of the family of what we in France call *gâteaux de voyage* (cakes that keep). This means that (apart from a small handful of the recipes) the cakes will keep for several days and, as a result, can be made in advance. Not to mention the fact that you can bake these cakes with a huge range of flavours, in a myriad of ways, and with a host of different texture and taste combinations.

The result of testing more than 200 recipes is now before you. The final selection of 56 recipes has been arranged in eight chapters, allowing you to choose according to the season, or to what takes your fancy, or by the ingredients in your store cupboard.

Before you begin, check out my list of the equipment required for all the recipes, and some useful tips on ingredients and techniques. All you need to do is turn the pages of this book and select your favourite recipes, making them exactly as I've done or adapting them according to your own personal taste. The main thing is to enjoy yourself – let's get baking!

BEFORE YOU START

BASIC EQUIPMENT 12

INGREDIENTS 14

TECHNIQUES 16

BASIC EQUIPMENT

WHAT YOU NEED

The aim of this book is to give you easy recipes that require the minimum of equipment, so you don't have to buy extra things. Here is a complete list of all the equipment needed.

1 LOAF TIN,
measuring 20 × 8 × 8 cm (8 × 3¼ × 3¼ inches)

1 LOAF TIN WITH REMOVABLE CYLINDER INSERT,
measuring 20 × 8 × 8 cm (8 × 3¼ × 3¼ inches)

MIXING BOWLS

HAND WHISK

RUBBER SPATULA

WIRE COOLING RACK

Extra equipment only needed for certain recipes:

ELECTRIC WHISK

DIGITAL KITCHEN THERMOMETER

2 SAUCEPANS

BLENDER OR FOOD PROCESSOR

PIPING BAGS, with or without piping nozzles

BRUSH (FOR SOAKING SYRUP)

KITCHEN BLOWTORCH (OPTIONAL)

If you already have all this equipment in your kitchen, you can start making any recipe in this book.

HANDY CONVERSIONS

If you already have a loaf tin, but it isn't 20 cm (8 inches) long, simply adjust the quantities of ingredients in each recipe by multiplying them by the following amounts.

LENGTH OF LOAF TIN	MULTIPLY BY
18 cm (7 inches)	0.9
22 cm (8½ inches)	1.1
24 cm (9½ inches)	1.2
26 cm (10¼ inches)	1.3
28 cm (11 inches)	1.4
30 cm (12 inches)	1.5

INGREDIENTS

BASIC INGREDIENTS

The basic ingredients in these recipes are often the same.

Butter: Preferably unsalted.

Cream: Preferably 35% fat content, or at least 30% fat. Both whipping cream and double cream could be used.

Eggs: In the majority of my recipes, except those where the egg quantity is shown by weight, I give the number of units (1 egg, 1 egg yolk, and so on). I suggest using medium-sized eggs, weighing 50 g when removed from the shell.

Sugar: The sugars I use the majority of the time are caster sugar (most frequently), icing sugar and light brown soft sugar. For some recipes, I also use muscovado, a dark brown, partially refined cane sugar, which is more aromatic than ordinary sugar.

Baking powder.

ADDITIONAL INGREDIENTS

These ingredients are used in some of the recipes, but are not essential.

Fruit purées: I use fruit purées containing 10% sugar.

Dairy products: Yogurt, mascarpone, ricotta, cream cheese (such as Philadelphia).

Nuts: Hazelnuts, almonds, pecans, pistachios, pine nuts.

Coffee: Instant or espresso.

Vanilla: Most of the time I use a vanilla pod or liquid extract.

Spreads.

Spices.

CHOCOLATE

This ingredient deserves an entire paragraph! In each recipe using chocolate, I've specified which type (dark, milk, white, blonde) as well as the percentage of cacao it should contain. If you want to use the same chocolate as me, I buy mine from Valrhona and below are the names of the different chocolates and the percentage of cacao they contain.

Dark chocolate with 66% cacao: Caraïbe.

Dark chocolate with 70% cacao: Guanaja.

Milk chocolate with 46% cacao: Bahibé.

Milk chocolate with 40% cacao: Jivara.

Milk chocolate with 35% cacao, flavoured with hazelnuts: Azelia.

Blonde chocolate: Dulcey.

White chocolate: Ivoire.

For best results when making the recipes, all the ingredients should be at room temperature.

TECHNIQUES

BASIC TECHNIQUES

In addition to allowing ingredients to come to room temperature, it is important that their condition matches that stated in the ingredients list (such as butter being melted or softened) and that they are added in the order stated in the method. With butter, in particular, take care not to add it when it is too hot – once melted, it must be left to cool to room temperature or until lukewarm. When 'softened butter' is indicated, the butter must be extremely soft and beaten with the sugar until creamy, or your cake batter may form lumps when the eggs are added. For many recipes, it is important to sift the flour and any other powdered ingredients to make a lighter, more homogeneous cake mixture.

To ensure an even, rounded top to your cake, there are two options:

Spoon a little very soft butter into a piping bag fitted with a tiny nozzle (about 3 mm/⅛ inch). If using a disposable bag, snip off the tip. Pipe a line of butter lengthways down the middle of the batter (see photograph, opposite). As the butter melts during baking, it will allow the cake to open up in the centre and rise evenly.

Or, after your cake has been baking for about 15 minutes, remove it from the oven and push the tip of a pointed knife into the centre. Next, run the tip down its entire length so it opens evenly and puffs up during the remaining baking time.

Let's move on to marbled cakes, which are a special case. These are my tips for achieving attractive marbling.

Some cake batters need to be chilled or rested in the refrigerator or a cool place before they are baked. Don't skip this step.

Use piping bags or freezer bags to pipe in the different-coloured mixtures so you get more even marbling.

Once the batters have been spooned into the piping bags, pipe a line of one of them, 2–3 cm (¾–1¼ inches) in diameter, down the centre of the tin, running the length of it. Pipe another one of the same size with the other batter on top. Repeat piping alternate lines of the batters, each one on top of the previous one, until both batters are used up, tapping the bottom of the tin on the work surface from time to time so the batters spread out in the tin. That's all you need do. There's no need to swirl a knife through the batters – the marbling will take care of itself when the cake rises in the oven.

If you don't have any piping bags or freezer bags, you can add the batters to the tin using two spoons, still following the same technique as above.

BAKING

Using a tin that has first been buttered and floured or lined with baking parchment will make turning out easy.

The secret of a successful cake is to bake it in an oven that is not too hot. The ideal temperature is usually 160ºC (325ºF), Gas Mark 3, with some exceptions. Depending on the recipe, cooking times can vary from 45 minutes–1½ hours, but it also depends on your oven. It is a good idea to check if a cake is cooked by pushing the tip of a pointed knife into the middle of it; the knife must come out dry (apart from recipes for a cheesecake, brownie or fondant).

USING A LOAF TIN WITH A CYLINDER INSERT AND FILLING THE CAKE

Before adding your batter to the tin, ensure that both the tin and the cylinder insert are well greased and floured.

Cakes baked in a tin with a cylinder insert need to be turned out from the tin slightly differently. After baking, let cool, then carefully twist and pull out the insert before turning out the cake as usual and leaving it to cool completely.

To fill the cavity, spoon the ganache, caramel or cream into a piping bag without a nozzle. Stand the cake upright on a tray, on one short end so that the bottom of the cavity is 'closed' and the cavity opening is on top. Pipe the filling into the hole until it is completely filled, then transfer the cake to the refrigerator until the filling has set.

STORING

Cakes that keep well (the *gâteaux de voyage* that I mentioned earlier) can be stored at room temperature for several days. Wait until they are completely cool, then tightly wrap in clingfilm. Of course, this does not apply to all cakes – some, such as the Creamy Cheesecake Loaf, Tiramisu Cake and Paris-Brest Cake (see pages 149, 146 and 158), need to be kept in the refrigerator. Where a certain cake does need to be kept chilled, I have indicated that in the recipe.

THE ICONS

SERVES

PREPARATION TIME

RESTING/CHILLING/COOLING TIME

COOKING TIME

BASIC RECIPES

HOW TO MAKE CHOCOLATE ICING	22
DARK CHOCOLATE ICING	24
DARK CHOCOLATE AND NUT ICING	24
MILK CHOCOLATE ICING	25
MILK CHOCOLATE AND NUT ICING	25
BLONDE CHOCOLATE ICING	26
BLONDE CHOCOLATE AND NUT ICING	26
HAZELNUT PRALINE	27
NUT BUTTERS	28

HOW TO MAKE CHOCOLATE ICING

You can use this easy method to make many kinds of chocolate icing (see pages 24–26 for ingredients).

For chocolate icing, always start by melting the chocolate gently in a bain-marie (a heatproof bowl set over a pan of gently simmering water, ensuring the base of the bowl does not touch the water) or in the microwave, keeping a close eye on it so it doesn't get too hot.

Remove the chocolate from the heat and add the oil.
Next, depending on the recipe, add the chopped nuts.

Leave the icing to cool until the temperature reaches about 35ºC (95ºF) before using it to decorate a cold cake. To ensure the icing sets more quickly, you can put the cake in the freezer for a few minutes before icing it.

When you are ready to ice the cake, place it on a wire rack set over a tray, board or large plate, so that you can scoop up and reuse any excess icing that rolls off.

Icing can be stored in the refrigerator for 6–8 weeks. To use it for your next cake, simply re-melt it gently.

DARK CHOCOLATE ICING

250 g (8 oz) dark chocolate with 66% cacao

3 tablespoons neutral oil, such as grapeseed

See page 22 for method.

DARK CHOCOLATE AND NUT ICING

250 g (8 oz) dark chocolate with 66% cacao

3 tablespoons neutral oil, such as grapeseed

50 g (2 oz) nuts, finely chopped

See page 22 for method.

MILK CHOCOLATE ICING

250 g (8 oz) milk chocolate with 40% cacao

2 tablespoons plus 1 teaspoon neutral oil, such as grapeseed

See page 22 for method.

MILK CHOCOLATE AND NUT ICING

250 g (8 oz) milk chocolate with 40% cacao

2 tablespoons plus 1 teaspoon neutral oil, such as grapeseed

50 g (2 oz) nuts, finely chopped

See page 22 for method.

BLONDE CHOCOLATE ICING

250 g (8 oz) blonde chocolate

2 tablespoons neutral oil, such as grapeseed

See page 22 for method.

BLONDE CHOCOLATE AND NUT ICING

250 g (8 oz) blonde chocolate

50 ml (2 fl oz) neutral oil, such as grapeseed

30 g (1¼ oz) nuts, finely chopped

See page 22 for method.

HAZELNUT PRALINE

Praline will keep for several months in a jar with a tight-fitting lid at room temperature.

300 g (10 oz) hazelnuts (from Piedmont, if possible)

65 ml (2¼ fl oz) water

200 g (7 oz) caster sugar

1 large pinch of sea salt flakes

Preheat the oven to 150ºC (300ºF), Gas Mark 2.

Line a shallow baking sheet with baking parchment and spread out the hazelnuts on it. Roast them in the oven for 15–20 minutes.

Pour the water into a large saucepan, then add the sugar. Bring to the boil, stirring until the sugar dissolves, then tip in the hazelnuts. Stir constantly with a spatula. The hazelnuts will first of all become covered with a white film before they caramelize. When they are well caramelized, scrape them out of the saucepan onto a baking sheet lined with baking parchment and leave them to cool completely.

When the hazelnuts are cold, transfer them to a food processor and grind finely into praline.

Stir in the sea salt flakes then transfer the praline to a jar for storage.

NUT BUTTERS

Nut butters will keep for several months in a jar with a tight-fitting lid at room temperature.

300 g (10 oz) nuts of your choice

Preheat the oven to 150ºC (300ºF), Gas Mark 2.

Line a shallow baking sheet with baking parchment and spread out the hazelnuts on it. Roast them in the oven for 15–20 minutes.

Let the nuts cool before transferring to a powerful blender or food processor and grinding them to a smooth paste. The grinding time will vary depending on the type of nut chosen.

THE CLASSICS

CLASSIC FRENCH YOGURT CAKE 34
VANILLA AND MUSCOVADO 37
CLOUD CAKE 38
RUM AND VANILLA 41
SALTED CARAMEL 42
SPECULOOS SPECIAL 45

SIMPLE RECIPES, TIMELESS FLAVOURS

I'm opening this book with the classic French yogurt cake recipe. It's an institution in France – the first thing that springs to mind at the word 'cake'. The recipe is swiftly followed by five others that are just as easy to prepare, and will take you on a flavour journey from Réunion Island to Belgium via Brittany. These simple classics are a great way to treat yourself, whatever your favourite flavour!

CLASSIC FRENCH YOGURT CAKE

 **Serves** 6-8

 **Preparation time:** 10 minutes

 **Cooking time:** 1 hour

In my native France, this is the most classic cake recipe there is, the one everyone knows – the yogurt cake! The recipe is very simple and quick and can be adapted to suit all tastes and the contents of your store cupboard. To give you a couple of examples, you can replace some of the neutral-flavoured oil with olive oil to produce a slightly more pronounced taste, or add your favourite flavouring, such as vanilla, orange blossom water, citrus zest or chocolate chips. Endless possibilities await, so let's go!

CAKE BATTER

- a little butter for greasing the tin and piping
- 185 g (6½ oz) plain flour, sifted, plus extra for dusting the tin
- 125 g (4 oz) natural yogurt
- 210 g (7¼ oz) light brown soft sugar
- 2 eggs
- 100 ml (3½ fl oz) neutral oil, such as grapeseed
- 6 g (1¼ teaspoons) baking powder

Preheat the oven to 160°C (325°F), Gas Mark 3. Butter and flour your loaf tin.

Whisk together the yogurt and sugar.

Add the eggs, one at a time, whisking after each addition.

Whisk in the oil, then fold in the flour and baking powder.

When you have a smooth batter, transfer it to the loaf tin. Pipe a line of butter down the middle of the batter (see page 16), then bake the cake for 1 hour.

Turn the cake out onto a wire rack and leave to cool.

VANILLA AND MUSCOVADO

 **Serves** 6–8    **Preparation time:** 20 minutes    **Cooking time:** 50 minutes

Another cake with a classic flavour, this time vanilla. In this recipe, it is combined with the subtle fragrance of muscovado sugar, which makes the cake flavourful and very moist. If you do not have any muscovado in your store cupboard, you can, of course, replace it with classic caster sugar.

CAKE BATTER

- 120 g (4 oz) butter, softened, plus extra for greasing the tin and piping
- 200 g (7 oz) plain flour, sifted, plus extra for dusting the tin
- 140 g (4½ oz) muscovado sugar (or see recipe introduction)
- 1 vanilla pod, split lengthways and seeds scraped out
- 4 eggs
- 7 g (1½ teaspoons) baking powder
- 50 ml (2 fl oz) whipping cream

Preheat the oven to 160ºC (325ºF), Gas Mark 3. Butter and flour your loaf tin.

Beat the butter with the sugar and vanilla seeds.

Add the eggs, one at a time, beating after each addition.

Fold in the sifted flour and baking powder.

Stir in the cream.

Transfer the batter to the loaf tin. Pipe a line of butter down the middle of the batter (see page 16), then bake the cake for 50 minutes.

When the cake comes out of the oven, leave it to cool for a few minutes before turning it out onto a wire rack to cool completely.

CLOUD CAKE

 **Serves** 6-8

 **Preparation time:** 20 minutes

 **Cooking time:** 25 minutes

This recipe is ideal for using up leftover egg whites. It has earned its name because its meringue base gives it an extremely moist and light texture. You can flavour the cake with spices or citrus zests as you wish.

CAKE BATTER

75 g (3 oz) butter, plus extra for greasing the tin

1 vanilla pod, split lengthways and seeds scraped out, or ½ tonka bean, grated, or the finely grated zest of 1 lemon

4 egg whites (about 130 g/4¼ oz)

165 g (5½ oz) light brown soft sugar, plus extra for dusting the tin

115 g (3¾ oz) plain flour, sifted

Preheat the oven to 180°C (350°F), Gas Mark 4.

Melt the butter along with the vanilla seeds, grated tonka bean or lemon zest. Leave to cool.

In a spotlessly clean bowl, whisk the egg whites with the sugar until you have a smooth, shiny meringue.

Using a spatula, carefully fold the sifted flour into the meringue, followed by the cooled melted butter.

Butter your loaf tin and dust it with sugar. Transfer the batter to the tin, then bake the cake for 25 minutes.

When the cake comes out of the oven, leave it to cool for a few minutes before turning it out onto a wire rack to cool completely.

RUM AND VANILLA

 Serves 6–8

 **Preparation time:** 20 minutes

 Cooking time: 50 minutes

After the classic vanilla cake comes the adult version, which combines vanilla with rum. I use an amber rum, which will not only give the cake a fuller flavour but will also fill your kitchen with its aroma while the cake is baking.

CAKE BATTER

- 50 g (2 oz) butter, plus extra for greasing the tin and piping
- 200 g (7 oz) plain flour, sifted, plus extra for dusting the tin
- 3 eggs
- 180 g (6 oz) light brown soft sugar
- 1 vanilla pod, split lengthways and seeds scraped out
- 50 ml (2 fl oz) amber rum
- 6 g (1¼ teaspoons) baking powder
- 50 ml (2 fl oz) whipping cream

Preheat the oven to 160ºC (325ºF), Gas Mark 3. Butter and flour your loaf tin.

Melt the butter, then leave it to cool until lukewarm.

Whisk the eggs together with the sugar until thickened and fluffy, then add the vanilla seeds and rum.

Fold in the sifted flour and baking powder, then fold in the lukewarm melted butter and the cream.

Transfer the batter to the loaf tin. Pipe a line of butter down the middle of the batter (see page 16), then bake the cake for 50 minutes.

When the cake comes out of the oven, leave it to cool for a few minutes before turning it out onto a wire rack to cool completely.

SALTED CARAMEL

 Serves 6–8    **Preparation time:** 40 minutes   **Cooking time:** 55 minutes

In this richly flavoured cake, salted caramel is used not just as a filling but is also drizzled over the top to make it even more indulgent. For this cake, you will need a loaf tin with a cylinder insert.

SALTED CARAMEL

300 g (10 oz) caster sugar

200 ml (7 fl oz) whipping cream

90 g (3¼ oz) butter, diced

1 large pinch of sea salt flakes

CAKE BATTER

60 g (2¼ oz) softened butter, plus extra for greasing the tin and piping

200 g (7 oz) plain flour, sifted, plus extra for dusting the tin

3 eggs

6 g (1¼ teaspoons) baking powder

90 ml (3¼ fl oz) whipping cream

Make a dry caramel by adding the sugar a little at a time to a saucepan set over a medium heat. At the same time, heat the cream in a separate pan. When the caramel is a rich amber colour, gradually pour the cream into it, whisking constantly. Add the diced butter, mix well and leave on the heat for another 5 minutes. Take the saucepan off the heat, add the salt, then leave the caramel to cool.

Preheat the oven to 160°C (325°F), Gas Mark 3. Butter and flour both your loaf tin and the cylinder insert, and fit the insert into the tin (see page 18).

Next, prepare the cake batter. Beat the softened butter with 250 g (8 oz) of the cold caramel (keep the rest of the caramel for the filling and decoration). Beat in the eggs, one at a time, followed by the sifted flour and baking powder. Finally, stir in the cream.

Transfer the batter to the loaf tin with the insert in place. Pipe a line of butter down the middle of the batter (see page 16), then bake the cake for 55 minutes.

When the cake comes out of the oven, leave it to cool for a few minutes before removing the insert (see page 18) and turning the cake out onto a wire rack. When it is completely cold, fill the centre with caramel (see page 18), then pipe or drizzle the rest decoratively over the top of the cake.

SPECULOOS SPECIAL

 Serves 6–8    Preparation time: 30 minutes    Cooking time: 55 minutes

This Belgian-inspired cake not only makes use of the speculoos spread, but also the broken biscuits and spice mix (which you can buy online). It pays tribute to the delicious little speculoos biscuit, also known as Biscoff, which is so popular at coffee time.

CAKE BATTER

75 g (3 oz) softened butter, plus extra for greasing the tin and piping

135 g (4¼ oz) plain flour, sifted, plus extra for dusting the tin

65 g (2½ oz) caster sugar

190 g (6½ oz) speculoos (Biscoff) spread

1 teaspoon speculoos spice mix

3 eggs

6 g (1¼ teaspoons) baking powder

85 ml (3¼ fl oz) whipping cream

30 g (1¼ oz) speculoos (Biscoff) biscuits, crushed into a powder with some small pieces remaining

FOR DECORATION

75 g (3 oz) speculoos (Biscoff) spread

10 g (½ oz) speculoos (Biscoff) biscuits, broken into small pieces

Preheat the oven to 160ºC (325ºF), Gas Mark 3. Butter and flour your loaf tin.

For the cake batter, beat together the butter and the sugar, then stir in the speculoos spread, the spice mix and the eggs, one at a time.

Mix in the sifted flour and baking powder, followed by the cream.

Finally, add the crushed biscuit powder.

Transfer the batter to the loaf tin, pipe a line of butter down the middle of the batter (see page 16), then bake the cake for 55 minutes.

When the cake comes out of the oven, leave it to cool for a few minutes before turning it out onto a wire rack to cool completely.

When the cake is cold, cover the top with the speculoos spread, then decorate with small pieces of speculoos biscuit.

VIVE LE CHOCOLAT!

HAZELNUT GIANDUJA 51

IRRESISTIBLE MARSHMALLOW 53

CHOCOLATE FONDANT 57

AZTEC HOT CHOCOLATE 58

MOCHA 60

THE ULTIMATE CHOCOLATE BROWNIE 63

NOSTALGIC CHOCOLATE AND HAZELNUT SPREAD CAKE 64

CHOCOLATE TAKES CENTRE STAGE

Whether combined with hazelnuts, coffee or spices, soft, melting or in a brownie, alone or accompanied by marshmallows or a spread, chocolate is a hit with almost everyone. That's why I've put together a selection of my favourite chocolate recipes. You may prefer dark or milk chocolate, in simple or more elaborate recipes, by itself or combined with other flavours. Whatever the case, you will find what you are looking for in this chapter!

HAZELNUT GIANDUJA

 **Serves** 6–8  **Preparation time:** 45 minutes 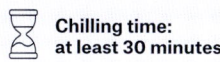 **Chilling time:** at least 30 minutes  **Cooking time:** 1 hour

Gianduja is praline's Italian cousin and is made with hazelnuts, milk chocolate and sugar. It is available to buy ready-made, but the advantage of making your own (provided you have a sufficiently powerful food processor) is that you can vary the chocolate to your own personal taste – for example, by using a milk chocolate that has a higher or lower percentage of cacao, or even dark chocolate for a less sweet result. The gianduja can be prepared several hours or days ahead, in which case melt it in a bain-marie before using. For this recipe, you will need a loaf tin with a cylinder insert.

GIANDUJA

100 g (3½ oz) hazelnuts

100 g (3½ oz) icing sugar

100 g (3½ oz) milk chocolate with 40% cacao, chopped

CAKE BATTER

60 g (2¼ oz) softened butter, plus extra for greasing the tin and piping

125 g (4 oz) plain flour, sifted, plus extra for dusting the tin

100 g (3½ oz) caster sugar

4 eggs

250 g (8 oz) gianduja (see above)

60 g (2¼ oz) ground hazelnuts

6 g (1¼ teaspoons) baking powder

60 ml (2¼ fl oz) whipping cream

2 tablespoons milk

continues overleaf >>>

To make the gianduja, preheat the oven to 150ºC (300ºF), Gas Mark 2. Line a shallow baking sheet with baking parchment and spread out the hazelnuts on it. Roast them for 15–20 minutes. Leave to cool.

While the hazelnuts are roasting, melt the chocolate in a bain-marie without letting the temperature of it exceed 40ºC (104ºF).

Transfer the cooled nuts to a food processor and add the icing sugar. Grind until you have quite a wet paste (about 10–15 minutes), then add the melted chocolate and process again until the gianduja is evenly mixed.

To make the cake batter, butter and flour both your loaf tin and the cylinder insert, and fit the insert into the tin (see page 18). Beat the softened butter and sugar together. Whisk in the eggs, one at a time, until incorporated, followed by 250 g (8 oz) gianduja. Fold in the ground hazelnuts, then the sifted flour and baking powder. Finally, stir in the cream.

Transfer the batter to the loaf tin with the insert in place. Pipe a line of butter down the middle of the batter (see page 16), then chill in the refrigerator for at least 30 minutes.

Preheat the oven to 150ºC (300ºF), Gas Mark 2, then bake the cake for 1 hour.

HAZELNUT GIANDUJA (continued)

MILK CHOCOLATE AND HAZELNUT ICING

250 g (8 oz) milk chocolate with 40% cacao

2 tablespoons plus 1 teaspoon neutral oil, such as grapeseed

50 g (2 oz) hazelnuts, finely chopped

At the end of the cooking time, brush the top of the cake with the milk. Leave it to cool completely before removing the insert (see page 18) and turning the cake out.

While the cake cools, prepare the icing following the instructions on page 22.

Once the cake is completely cold, fill it with the gianduja (melting it first, if necessary, in a bain-marie). Place the cake on a wire rack and coat with the icing, spreading it over the top and down the sides. Refrigerate until the icing has set.

IRRESISTIBLE MARSHMALLOW

 Serves
6–8

 **Preparation time:**
1 hour

 Cooking time:
1 hour

 Chilling time:
30–40 minutes

This is the cake version of an irresistible French treat: a marshmallow teddy bear covered in a thin layer of crisp chocolate. This chocolate loaf cake is filled and topped with soft vanilla marshmallow, not to mention milk chocolate icing. Of course, you can make the recipe without the marshmallow and the icing for a more classic but still delicious chocolate cake. For this recipe, you will need a loaf tin with a cylinder insert.

CAKE BATTER

130 g (4¼ oz) butter, plus extra for greasing the tin and piping

150 g (5 oz) plain flour, sifted, plus extra for dusting the tin

150 g (5 oz) dark chocolate with 66% cacao

3 eggs

100 g (3½ oz) caster sugar

25 g (1 oz) unsweetened cocoa powder

6 g (1¼ teaspoons) baking powder

100 ml (3½ fl oz) whipping cream

3 tablespoons full-fat milk

100 g (3½ oz) milk chocolate with 35% cacao, chopped

SOAKING SYRUP

2 tablespoons plus 2 teaspoons full-fat milk

1 teaspoon unsweetened cocoa powder

2 teaspoons caster sugar

MILK CHOCOLATE ICING

25 g (1 oz) milk chocolate with 40% cacao

2 tablespoons plus 1 teaspoon neutral oil, such as grapeseed

continues overleaf >>>

Preheat the oven to 160ºC (325ºF), Gas Mark 3. Butter and flour both your loaf tin and the cylinder insert, and fit the insert into the tin (see page 18).

Melt the butter with the chocolate.

Whisk the eggs with the sugar until thickened and fluffy, then fold in the melted butter and chocolate. Next, fold in the sifted flour, cocoa and baking powder. Finally, add the cream and the milk, followed by the chopped milk chocolate.

Transfer the cake batter to the loaf tin with the insert in place and pipe a line of butter down the middle of the batter (see page 16). Bake the cake for 1 hour.

While the cake is baking, prepare the soaking syrup. Put the 3 ingredients into a small saucepan and bring to the boil.

When the cake comes out of the oven, brush the syrup over the top of it and leave it to cool in the tin.

Remove the insert and turn the cake out of the tin.

Prepare the milk chocolate icing following the instructions on page 22.

To make the marshmallow, soak the gelatine leaves in a large bowl of cold water. Heat the water, sugar and glucose syrup in a saucepan. When the temperature of the syrup reaches 110ºC (230ºF), begin whisking the egg whites in a mixing bowl. When the syrup reaches 130ºC (266ºF), squeeze out the gelatine leaves to remove excess water and add them to the syrup. Pour the syrup in a thin, steady stream into the egg whites, whisking constantly. Finally, add the vanilla. When the marshmallow is completely smooth, leave it to cool, then spoon it into a piping bag fitted with a plain 8mm (⅓ inch) nozzle.

IRRESISTIBLE MARSHMALLOW (continued)

VANILLA MARSHMALLOW

10 g (½ oz) (about 4) gelatine leaves

60 ml (2¼ fl oz) water

200 g (7 oz) caster sugar

2 tablespoons glucose syrup

60 g (2¼ oz) egg whites

2 tablespoons vanilla extract

neutral oil, for greasing

FOR DUSTING

icing sugar, for dusting

cornflour, for dusting

Fill the cavity in the cake with the marshmallow (see page 18), then place the cake in the freezer for 10–15 minutes to let the marshmallow set.

Line a baking sheet with lightly oiled clingfilm and pipe the rest of the marshmallow onto it in long strips. Leave the strips to set.

Mix equal parts of icing sugar and cornflour together in a bowl. When the marshmallow strips are set, cut them into mini marshmallows and roll them in the sugar and cornflour mixture.

Ice the cake and chill it in the refrigerator until the icing starts to set. Decorate with the mini marshmallows, then return the cake to the refrigerator until the icing is completely set.

CHOCOLATE FONDANT

 Serves 6-8

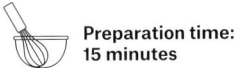 **Preparation time:** 15 minutes

 **Cooking time:** 33 minutes

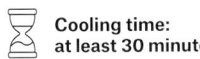 **Cooling time:** at least 30 minutes

Chocolate fondant is one of the great classics of French baking. It is often prepared as individual servings, but here I'm suggesting making it as a loaf cake to share. The cooking time will, of course, depend on your oven, but also on personal taste, depending on whether you prefer the fondant to be very runny in the centre or a little firmer.

CAKE BATTER

200 g (7 oz) butter, diced, plus extra for greasing the tin

50 g (2 oz) plain flour, sifted, plus extra for dusting the tin

190 g (6½ oz) dark chocolate with 66% cacao

1 pinch of salt

5 eggs

120 g (4 oz) light brown soft sugar

FOR DECORATION

1 pinch of sea salt flakes

Preheat the oven to 210°C (410°F), Gas Mark 6½. Butter and flour your loaf tin.

Melt the chocolate with the butter and then add the pinch of salt.

Whisk the eggs with the sugar until thickened and fluffy. Add the melted chocolate and butter, then fold in the sifted flour.

Transfer the batter to the loaf tin. Bake for 5 minutes, then reduce the oven temperature to 120°C (250°F), Gas Mark ½ and continue to bake for a further 28 minutes.

Leave the cake to cool in the tin for at least 30 minutes before turning it out. Serve with a pinch of sea salt flakes sprinkled on top.

AZTEC HOT CHOCOLATE

 Serves 6–8

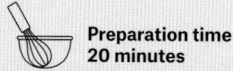 **Preparation time:** 20 minutes

 **Cooking time:** 1 hour

The best hot chocolate I have ever had was thick, spicy and very chocolaty. For this recipe, that memorable hot chocolate has been transformed into a cake made with chocolate that contains quite a high percentage of cacao, plus muscovado sugar, ground black pepper and a mix of spices. I've named it Aztec as a tribute to the people who prepared their chocolate using more spices than we are used to today. For added indulgence, you can serve the cake with a cloud of lightly sweetened whipped cream.

CAKE BATTER

- 140 g (4½ oz) butter, plus extra for greasing the tin and piping
- 180 g (6 oz) plain flour, sifted, plus extra for dusting the tin
- 170 g (5¾ oz) dark chocolate with 70% cacao
- 1 teaspoon *quatre épices* spice mix (buy online or make your own by grinding 1½ teaspoons black peppercorns, ¾ teaspoon ground nutmeg, ½ teaspoon ground cinnamon and ½ teaspoon ground cloves in a spice grinder)
- 1 teaspoon gingerbread spice mix
- 2 teaspoons sweet paprika
- ½ teaspoon ground ginger
- 2 teaspoons ground black pepper
- 3 eggs
- 150 g (5 oz) muscovado sugar
- 1 tablespoon vanilla extract
- 7 g (1½ teaspoons) baking powder
- 100 ml (3½ fl oz) whipping cream

SPICED MILK

- 2 tablespoons plus 1 teaspoon milk
- 1 teaspoon gingerbread spice mix
- ½ teaspoon ground black pepper

DARK CHOCOLATE ICING

- 250 g (8 oz) dark chocolate with 66% cacao
- 3 tablespoons neutral oil, such as grapeseed

Preheat the oven to 160°C (325°F), Gas Mark 3. Butter and flour your loaf tin.

To make the cake batter, melt the chocolate with the butter, then stir in the spices and the black pepper.

Whisk the eggs with the sugar and vanilla extract until thickened and fluffy. Fold in the melted spiced chocolate, followed by the sifted flour and baking powder. Finally, mix in the cream.

Transfer the batter to the loaf tin and pipe a line of butter down the centre of the batter (see page 16). Bake for 1 hour.

Shortly before the end of the cooking time, prepare the spiced milk. Mix the ingredients together, then brush the spiced milk over the top of the cake when it comes out of the oven. Wait until the cake has cooled before turning it out of the tin.

Prepare the dark chocolate icing following the instructions on page 22. Pour the icing over the cake (set over a wire rack if you want a neater finish) and leave until the icing has set.

MOCHA

 **Serves** 6-8   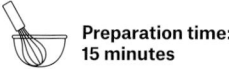 **Preparation time:** 15 minutes   **Cooking time:** 1 hour 10 minutes

The best way to end a meal is with a square of chocolate dipped in coffee. Chocolate and coffee make a classic and delicious combination, especially when accompanied by blonde chocolate icing, which complements the aroma of the coffee perfectly, as in this recipe. If you don't have time to prepare the icing, you can always add blonde chocolate chips directly to the cake batter.

CAKE BATTER

65 g (2½ oz) softened butter, plus extra for greasing the tin and piping

150 g (5 oz) plain flour, plus extra for dusting the tin

160 g (5½ oz) dark chocolate with 66% cacao

130 g (4¼ oz) caster sugar

3 eggs

12 g (½ oz) instant coffee granules

2 tablespoons cold espresso

25 g (1 oz) unsweetened cocoa powder

7 g (1½ teaspoons) baking powder

125 ml (4 fl oz) whipping cream

SOAKING SYRUP

4 teaspoons water

4 teaspoons sugar

4 teaspoons cold espresso

BLONDE CHOCOLATE ICING

250 g (8 oz) blonde chocolate

2 tablespoons neutral oil, such as grapeseed

Preheat the oven to 160ºC (325ºF), Gas Mark 3. Butter and flour your loaf tin.

To make the cake batter, melt the chocolate in a bain-marie.

Beat the softened butter with the sugar. Add the eggs, one at a time, beating each one in before adding the next. Stir in the melted chocolate and instant coffee, followed by the espresso. Sift in the flour, cocoa and baking powder, then fold in. Finish by stirring in the cream.

Transfer the batter to the loaf tin, then pipe a line of butter down the middle of the batter (see page 16). Bake the cake for 1 hour 10 minutes.

While the cake is baking, prepare the soaking syrup. Mix the 3 ingredients together in a small saucepan and bring to the boil. Alternatively, place in a microwave-safe bowl and heat in the microwave.

When the cake comes out of the oven, brush the hot syrup over it. Leave the cake to cool in the tin for a few minutes before turning it out onto a wire rack to cool completely.

Prepare the icing following the instructions on page 22. Pour the icing over the cold cake, spreading it over the top and sides in an even layer, and leave to set.

THE ULTIMATE CHOCOLATE BROWNIE

 Serves 6-8

 Preparation time: 20 minutes

 Cooking time: 35 minutes

 Cooling time: at least 30 minutes

Lovers of chocolate cake can often be divided into 'team fondant' and 'team brownie'. We've already had the Chocolate Fondant cake (see page 57), so here is the Brownie cake, which I've flavoured with tonka bean. It is, of course, optional, so if you are not crazy about tonka bean, you can add nuts or chocolate chips instead.

CAKE BATTER

- 200 g (7 oz) butter, diced, plus extra for greasing the tin
- 75 g (3 oz) plain flour, sifted, plus extra for dusting the tin
- 330 g (11 oz) dark chocolate with 66% cacao, chopped
- 4 eggs
- 120 g (4 oz) caster sugar
- 1 tonka bean, grated (optional; see recipe introduction)

Preheat the oven to 200ºC (400ºF), Gas Mark 6. Butter and flour your loaf tin.

Melt the chocolate with the butter.

Whisk the eggs with the sugar and grated tonka bean for about 10 minutes until the mixture is white and has tripled in volume. Add the melted chocolate and butter, followed by the sifted flour, folding the ingredients together gently with a spatula.

Transfer the batter to the loaf tin. Reduce the oven temperature to 150ºC (300ºF), Gas Mark 2 and bake for 35 minutes.

When the cake comes out of the oven, leave it to cool in the tin for 30 minutes before turning it out onto a wire rack to cool completely.

NOSTALGIC CHOCOLATE AND HAZELNUT SPREAD CAKE

 Serves 6–8  **Preparation time:** 30 minutes  **Cooking time:** 55 minutes

In this recipe, I revisit in cake form the ultimate childhood afternoon snack of a slice of bread covered with a generous layer of your favourite brand of chocolate and hazelnut spread. This recipe is very easy and perfect for both young and old.

CAKE BATTER

75 g (3 oz) softened butter, plus extra for greasing the tin and piping

135 g (4¼ oz) plain flour, sifted, plus extra for dusting the tin

65 g (2½ oz) caster sugar

190 g (6½ oz) chocolate and hazelnut spread

3 eggs

6 g (1¼ teaspoons) baking powder

50 ml (2 fl oz) whipping cream

30 g (1¼ oz) roasted hazelnuts, chopped

FOR DECORATION

65 g (2½ oz) chocolate and hazelnut spread

45 g (1¾ oz) roasted hazelnuts

Preheat the oven to 160°C (325°F), Gas Mark 3. Butter and flour your loaf tin.

To make the cake batter, beat the softened butter with the sugar. Stir in the chocolate and hazelnut spread, then beat in the eggs, one at a time. Mix in the sifted flour and baking powder, followed by the cream. Finally, stir in the chopped roasted hazelnuts.

Transfer the batter to the loaf tin. Pipe a line of butter down the middle of the batter (see page 16), then bake the cake for 55 minutes.

When it comes out of the oven, leave the cake to cool for a few minutes before turning it out onto a wire rack to cool completely.

When the cake is cold, spread the top with a layer of chocolate and hazelnut spread. Cut the roasted hazelnuts in half and press them on top for decoration, adding any crumbs of hazelnut from the chopping board too.

MARBLED TO PERFECTION

CLASSIC MARBLE CAKE	71
CHOCOLATE AND PISTACHIO MARBLE	72
ULTIMATE HAZELNUT GANACHE	74
MARBLED SUMMER FRUITS	76
TRIPLE CHOCOLATE MARBLE	79
MOGADOR MARBLE	80
COZY CINNAMON MARBLE	83
MATCHA MARBLE	86

BEAUTIFULLY BLENDED, DELICIOUSLY EASY

If your favourite cake is a marbled one, you're in for a real treat! I include the ever-popular chocolate and vanilla marbled cake, along with a host of chocolaty and nutty recipes. This is your chance to combine chocolate with a whole range of flavours, including vanilla (of course) but also pistachio, cinnamon, passion fruit and hazelnut. You'll also find recipes that don't contain chocolate, but are full of freshness and colour for more summery desserts.

See my tips for successful marbling on page 16.

CLASSIC MARBLE CAKE

 Serves 6-8

 **Preparation time:** 15 minutes

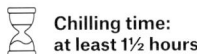 **Chilling time:** at least 1½ hours

 **Cooking time:** 1 hour 10 minutes

Let's begin this chapter on marbled cakes with the most popular of them all: chocolate and vanilla, which practically everyone has tried at some point in their lives. You can add an indulgent and sophisticated touch to this great classic by decorating it with the icing of your choice.

CAKE BATTER

130 g (4¼ oz) softened butter, plus extra for greasing the tin and piping

160 g (5½ oz) caster sugar

1 tablespoon vanilla extract

4 eggs

190 g (6½ oz) plain flour, sifted, plus extra for dusting the tin

7 g (1½ teaspoons) baking powder

85 ml (3¼ fl oz) whipping cream

15 g (½ oz) unsweetened cocoa powder

50 g (2 oz) dark chocolate chips

1 vanilla pod, split lengthways and seeds scraped out

Beat the butter with the sugar and vanilla extract. Add the eggs, one at a time, whisking each one in before adding the next, then fold in the sifted flour and baking powder. Finally, stir in 60 ml (2¼ fl oz) of the cream.

Divide the batter equally between 2 mixing bowls (each half of the batter should weigh about 375 g/12 oz). Mix the cocoa powder, the rest of the cream and the chocolate chips into one bowl of batter. Add the vanilla seeds to the second bowl.

Spoon each batter into a disposable piping bag and chill in the refrigerator for at least 1½ hours.

Preheat the oven to 160ºC (325ºF), Gas Mark 3. Butter and flour your loaf tin.

Snip the tips off the piping bags and pipe a line of the vanilla batter in the centre of the tin running the length of it, followed by a line of chocolate batter on top. Repeat piping lengths, alternating the batters until both have been used up (see my tips on page 16) and tapping the tin on the work surface to level out the batters.

Pipe a line of butter down the middle of the batter (see page 16), then bake the cake for 1 hour 10 minutes.

When the cake comes out of the oven, leave it to cool in the tin for a few minutes before turning it out onto a wire rack to cool completely.

CHOCOLATE AND PISTACHIO MARBLE

 Serves 6–8   **Preparation time:** 20 minutes   **Chilling time:** at least 30 minutes   **Cooking time:** 55 minutes

Pistachios go really well with a wide variety of ingredients, such as strawberry, raspberry, lemon and apricot, but chocolate makes the best match of all. This chocolate and pistachio marbled cake is just as easy to prepare as the traditional chocolate and vanilla one. I've left it un-iced deliberately so the chocolate does not overpower the slightly more subtle flavour of the pistachios. However, you can cover the cake with, for example, a dark chocolate and pistachio icing (see page 24) for a more stylish and indulgent finish, if you wish.

CAKE BATTER

- 60 g (2¼ oz) softened butter, plus extra for greasing the tin
- 175 g (6 oz) caster sugar
- 90 g (3¼ oz) Pistachio Butter (see page 28)
- 3 eggs
- 180 g (6 oz) plain flour, sifted, plus extra for dusting the tin
- 6 g (1¼ teaspoons) baking powder
- 85 ml (3¼ fl oz) whipping cream
- 100 ml (3½ fl oz) full-fat milk
- 25 g (1 oz) unsweetened cocoa powder

Beat together the softened butter and sugar, then stir in the pistachio butter. Add the eggs, one at a time, whisking in each one before adding the next. Stir in the sifted flour and baking powder, then finally the cream and 75 ml (3 fl oz) of the milk.

Divide the batter equally between 2 mixing bowls. Stir the cocoa and the remaining milk into one of them.

Spoon each batter into a disposable piping bag and chill in the refrigerator for at least 30 minutes.

Preheat the oven to 160°C (325°F), Gas Mark 3. Butter and flour your loaf tin.

Snip the tips off the piping bags and pipe a line of the chocolate batter in the centre of the tin running the length of it, followed by a line of pistachio batter on top. Repeat piping lengths, alternating the batters until both have been used up (see my tips on page 16) and tapping the tin on the work surface to level them out.

Bake the cake for 55 minutes.

When the cake comes out of the oven, turn it out onto a wire rack and leave it to cool.

ULTIMATE HAZELNUT GANACHE

 **Serves** 6–8    **Preparation time:** 1 hour 10 minutes    **Chilling time:** 1½–2 hours    **Cooking time:** 55 minutes

After vanilla and pistachio, it's time for the extremely popular hazelnut to take centre stage. I've used it for my 'ultimate' cake, the inspiration for which was the marbled cake of French pâtissier, Cyril Lignac. This marbled chocolate and hazelnut cake is filled with a creamy milk chocolate and hazelnut ganache, covered with his milk chocolate and hazelnut icing, with the finished cake sitting on a crunchy hazelnut base. For this recipe, you will need a loaf tin with a cylinder insert.

CAKE BATTER

50 g (2 oz) softened butter, plus extra for greasing the tin and piping

150 g (5 oz) caster sugar

80 g (3 oz) Hazelnut Butter (see page 28)

130 g (4¼ oz) eggs (about 2–3 large eggs), beaten

70 g (2¾ oz) ground hazelnuts

110 g (3¾ oz) plain flour, sifted, plus extra for dusting the tin

6 g (1¼ teaspoons) baking powder

90 ml (3¼ fl oz) whipping cream

65 ml (2¼ fl oz) full-fat milk

15 g (½ oz) unsweetened cocoa powder

FILLING

60 g (2¼ oz) milk chocolate with 40% cacao

65 g (2½ oz) Hazelnut Praline (see page 27)

50 ml (2 fl oz) whipping cream

10 g (½ oz) honey

20 g (¾ oz) butter, diced

To make the cake batter, beat the softened butter with the sugar and then stir in the hazelnut butter.

Add the eggs, a little at a time, whisking until each addition has been mixed in. Whisking constantly, add these ingredients in the following order: ground hazelnuts, sifted flour, baking powder, cream and milk.

Divide the batter equally between 2 mixing bowls and stir the cocoa powder into 1 of them. Spoon each batter into a disposable piping bag and chill in the refrigerator for 30 minutes.

Preheat the oven to 160ºC (325ºF), Gas Mark 3. Butter and flour both your loaf tin and the cylinder insert, and fit the insert into the tin (see page 18).

Snip the tips off the piping bags and pipe the batters alternately into the loaf tin with the insert in place (see page 16) until they are used up. Pipe a line of butter down the middle of the cake (see page 16) and bake for 55 minutes.

When the cake comes out of the oven, leave it to cool for a few minutes before removing the insert and turning the cake out onto a wire rack. Leave it to cool completely at room temperature.

Meanwhile, make the filling. Melt the chocolate, then stir in the praline. Heat the cream with the honey, then add the mixture, one-third at a time, to the chocolate and praline mixture, mixing well after each addition to make a smooth, shiny ganache. Finally, add the butter. When the ganache is evenly mixed, transfer it to the refrigerator for 30 minutes–1 hour. When it is still very creamy, spoon it into a piping bag and fill the cake with it (see page 18).

CRUNCHY HAZELNUT BASE

40 g (1½ oz) milk chocolate with 40% cacao

70 g (2¾ oz) Hazelnut Praline (see page 27)

40 g (1½ oz) *feuilletines* (thin crisp crêpes or crêpe dentelle, which can be sourced online), crumbled into small pieces

MILK CHOCOLATE AND HAZELNUT ICING

250 g (8 oz) milk chocolate with 40% cacao

2 tablespoons plus 1 teaspoon neutral oil, such as grapeseed oil

50 g (2 oz) hazelnuts, finely chopped

To make the crunchy hazelnut base, melt the chocolate, then add the praline and crumbled *feuilletines*. Mix well and spread the mixture over a sheet of baking parchment cut to the size of the loaf tin and placed on a board. Sit the cake on top so it sticks to the base, trimming the base, if necessary, so it is level with the cake. Place in the refrigerator while you make the icing.

Finally, make the icing following the instructions on page 22. Transfer the cake to a wire rack and pour the icing over, spreading it to cover the top and sides. Return it to the refrigerator until ready to serve.

MARBLED SUMMER FRUITS

 Serves 6–8   **Preparation time:** 25 minutes   **Chilling time:** at least 1½ hours   **Cooking time:** 1 hour

It's midsummer and you're craving a cake. Well, why not? This refreshing combination of raspberries and lime is exactly what you need. Raspberries also go very well with lemons and other citrus fruits such as yuzu, so feel free to ring the changes by using the zest or juice of one of these alternatives.

LIME CAKE BATTER

- 15 g (½ oz) butter, plus extra for greasing the tin and piping
- 75 g (3 oz) caster sugar
- finely grated zest of 2 organic or unwaxed limes
- 1 egg
- 25 ml (1 fl oz) freshly squeezed lime juice
- 70 g (2¾ oz) plain flour, sifted, plus extra for dusting the tin
- 2 g (heaped ⅓ teaspoon) baking powder
- 1 tablespoon whipping cream

RASPBERRY CAKE BATTER

- 30 g (1¼ oz) butter
- 2 eggs
- 75 g (3 oz) caster sugar
- 110 g (3¾ oz) raspberry purée
- 110 g (3¾ oz) plain flour, sifted
- 3 g (heaped ½ teaspoon) baking powder
- 25 ml (1 fl oz) whipping cream

SOAKING SYRUP

- 15 g (½ oz) raspberry purée
- 4 teaspoons freshly squeezed lime juice

To make the lime cake batter, melt the butter and leave it to cool to lukewarm.

Beat the sugar with the lime zest, then whisk in the egg until thickened and fluffy. Stir in the lime juice, followed by the sifted flour and baking powder. Finally, pour in the lukewarm butter along with the cream, mixing well. Spoon the batter into a disposable piping bag and chill in the refrigerator for at least 1½ hours.

For the raspberry cake batter, melt the butter and leave it to cool to lukewarm. Whisk the eggs with the sugar until thickened and fluffy, then add the raspberry purée. Fold in the sifted flour and baking powder, followed by the lukewarm butter and cream. Spoon the batter into a disposable piping bag and chill in the refrigerator for at least 1½ hours.

Make the soaking syrup by stirring the 2 ingredients together.

Preheat the oven to 160ºC (325ºF), Gas Mark 3. Butter and flour your loaf tin.

Snip the tips off the piping bags and pipe lines of the lime and raspberry batters alternately in layers in the centre of the tin running the length of it (see page 16), until both have been used up. Pipe a line of butter down the middle of the batter (see page 16), then bake the cake for 1 hour.

As soon as the cake comes out of the oven, brush it with the soaking syrup. Leave the cake to cool completely before turning it out.

TRIPLE CHOCOLATE MARBLE

 Serves 6–8  **Preparation time:** 35 minutes **Cooking time:** 1 hour 25 minutes

After a little fruit, here is a marbled cake for chocolate devotees, made with three successive layers of white, milk and dark chocolate batters and covered with blonde chocolate icing. You can use dark or milk chocolate icing (see pages 24 and 25) if you prefer.

CAKE BATTER

- 120 g (4 oz) butter, plus extra for greasing the tin and piping
- 150 g (5 oz) plain flour, sifted, plus extra for dusting the tin
- 95 g (3¼ oz) white chocolate
- 80 g (3 oz) milk chocolate with 40% cacao
- 65 g (2½ oz) dark chocolate with 66% cacao
- 145 ml (¼ pint) full-fat milk
- 3 eggs
- 100 g (3½ oz) caster sugar
- 5 g (1 teaspoon) baking powder

BLONDE CHOCOLATE ICING

- 250 g (8 oz) blonde chocolate
- 2 tablespoons neutral oil, such as grapeseed

Preheat the oven to 160°C (325°F), Gas Mark 3. Butter and flour your loaf tin.

Melt each chocolate in a separate bowl.

Melt the butter with 100 ml (3½ fl oz) of the milk, then leave until it has cooled to lukewarm.

Whisk the eggs with the sugar until thickened and fluffy. Add the sifted flour and baking powder, followed by the lukewarm butter and milk, then fold everything together until evenly combined.

Divide the batter equally between 3 mixing bowls, then mix 1 type of melted chocolate into each. Stir 4 teaspoons of milk into the milk chocolate batter and the remaining milk into the dark chocolate batter.

Spoon each batter into a disposable piping bag. Snip the tips off the piping bags and pipe the batters alternately in lines in the centre of the tin running the length of it, until all 3 have been used up (see page 16). Pipe a line of butter down the middle of the batter (see page 16), then bake the cake for 1 hour 25 minutes.

When it comes out of the oven, turn the cake out onto a wire rack and leave it to cool.

Meanwhile, make the icing following the instructions on page 22. Pour the icing over the cold cake, spreading it over the top and down the sides. Leave until the icing has set.

MOGADOR MARBLE

 Serves 6–8  **Preparation time:** 45 minutes   **Cooking time:** 55 minutes

Milk chocolate and passion fruit is a combination macaron lovers will recognize. Known in France as 'Mogador', it's a match made in heaven that has found itself in the spotlight thanks to French pâtissier Pierre Hermé's incomparable macarons. The sweetness of the chocolate with the hint of acidity from the passion fruit make this cake quite addictive – you have been warned!

PASSION FRUIT CAKE BATTER

40 g (1½ oz) butter, plus extra for greasing the tin and piping

2 eggs

50 g (2 oz) caster sugar

100 g (3½ oz) passion fruit purée

100 g (3½ oz) plain flour, sifted, plus extra for dusting the tin

3 g (heaped ½ teaspoon) baking powder

25 ml (1 fl oz) whipping cream

MILK CHOCOLATE CAKE BATTER

75 g (3 oz) milk chocolate with 46% cacao

25 g (1 oz) butter

2 eggs

50 g (2 oz) caster sugar

100 g (3½ oz) plain flour

3 g (heaped ½ teaspoon) baking powder

60 ml (2¼ fl oz) whipping cream

continues overleaf >>>

For the passion fruit cake batter, melt the butter and leave it to cool to lukewarm.

Whisk the eggs with the sugar until thickened and fluffy, then add the passion fruit purée. Fold in the sifted flour and baking powder, followed by the lukewarm butter and the cream.

Spoon the batter into a disposable piping bag and chill in the refrigerator while you prepare the chocolate batter.

To make the chocolate cake batter, melt the butter and chocolate together, then leave to cool until lukewarm. Whisk the eggs with the sugar until thick, then add the melted butter and chocolate, the sifted flour and baking powder and finally the cream. Fold everything together until evenly mixed, then spoon the batter into a disposable piping bag.

Preheat the oven to 160ºC (325ºF), Gas Mark 3. Butter and flour your loaf tin.

Snip the tips off the piping bags and pipe the batters alternately in lines in the centre of the tin running the length of it (see page 16), until both have been used up. Pipe a line of butter down the middle of the batter (see page 16), then bake the cake for 55 minutes.

MOGADOR MARBLE (continued)

SOAKING SYRUP

25 g (1 oz) passion fruit purée

25 ml (1 fl oz) water

2 teaspoons caster sugar

MILK CHOCOLATE ICING

250 g (8 oz) milk chocolate with 40% cacao

2 tablespoons plus 1 teaspoon neutral oil, such as grapeseed

FOR DECORATION

1 passion fruit, pulp scooped out

Make the soaking syrup by bringing the ingredients to the boil in a saucepan. When the cake comes out of the oven, brush the syrup over it and leave the cake to cool completely in the tin before turning it out onto a wire rack.

Make the milk chocolate icing following the instructions on page 22. Pour the icing over the cold cake. Just before it has set, spoon a little passion fruit pulp on top for decoration.

COZY CINNAMON MARBLE

 Serves 6-8  **Preparation time:** 1 hour 10 minutes   **Chilling and freezing time:** 1 hour 10 minutes  **Cooking time:** 1 hour 10 minutes

This recipe is perfect for autumn evenings, when the days are drawing in and all you want to do is snuggle up under a blanket with a generous slice of cake. If you like cinnamon, follow the recipe as is. If not, replace the cinnamon with vanilla or grated tonka bean. For this recipe, you will need a loaf tin with a cylinder insert.

CAKE BATTER

120 g (4 oz) softened butter, plus extra for greasing the tin and piping

200 g (7 oz) caster sugar

1 large pinch of salt

7 g (1½ teaspoons) baking powder

2 eggs

200 g (7 oz) plain flour, sifted, plus extra for dusting the tin

3 g (heaped ½ teaspoon) ground cinnamon

200 ml (7 fl oz) whipping cream

25 g (1 oz) unsweetened cocoa powder, sifted, plus extra for dusting

SOAKING SYRUP

60 ml (2¼ fl oz) water

15 g (½ oz) caster sugar

1 pinch of ground cinnamon

CARAMEL, CINNAMON AND CHOCOLATE CREAM

50 g (2 oz) caster sugar

60 ml (2¼ fl oz) whipping cream

1 pinch of ground cinnamon

1 egg yolk

15 g (½ oz) butter, diced

50 g (2 oz) milk chocolate with 40% cacao, chopped

1 pinch of salt

continues overleaf >>>

To make the batters, beat together the softened butter, sugar and salt. Stir in the baking powder, then beat in the eggs, one at a time.

Spoon one-third of the batter (about 140 g/4½ oz) into a separate mixing bowl. Stir together 75 g (3 oz) of the flour with the cinnamon, and stir it into this smaller amount of batter, followed by 65 ml (2¼ fl oz) of the cream.

Combine the remaining flour with the cocoa and stir it into the larger batter quantity, followed by the remaining cream.

Spoon each batter into a disposable piping bag and chill in the refrigerator for 30 minutes.

Preheat the oven to 160°C (325°F), Gas Mark 3. Butter and flour both your loaf tin and the cylinder insert, and fit the insert into the tin (see page 18).

Snip the tips off the piping bags and pipe lines of the 2 batters alternately in the centre of the tin with the insert in place, running the length of it, until both have been used up (see page 16). Finish by piping a line of butter down the middle of the batter (see page 16), then bake the cake for 1 hour and 10 minutes.

To make the soaking syrup, bring the water, sugar and cinnamon to the boil. When the cake is cooked, remove it from the oven and brush the syrup over it. Leave the cake to cool completely before removing the insert and turning the cake out.

COZY CINNAMON MARBLE (continued)

MILK CHOCOLATE AND HAZELNUT ICING

250 g (8 oz) milk chocolate with 40% cacao

2 tablespoons plus 1 teaspoon neutral oil, such as grapeseed

50 g (2 oz) hazelnuts, finely chopped

CHANTILLY CREAM

100 ml (3½ fl oz) whipping cream

4 teaspoons icing sugar

To make the caramel, cinnamon and chocolate cream, heat the sugar in a saucepan to make a dry caramel. At the same time, heat the cream and cinnamon in a separate saucepan. Put the egg yolk in a heatproof mixing bowl. Pour the hot cream over the caramel, stirring briskly. Remove from the heat and leave to cool for a few minutes, then whisk the mixture into the egg yolk.

Transfer the mixture to a saucepan and cook, in the same way as for making a custard, until the temperature reaches 85ºC (185ºF). Take the saucepan off the heat, add the butter, chocolate and salt, and stir until evenly combined. If necessary, blend until completely smooth. Press clingfilm over the surface and refrigerate until needed.

When the cake is completely cold, spoon the caramel, cinnamon and chocolate cream into a piping bag and fill the cake with it (see page 18). Put the cake in the freezer for at least 30–40 minutes so it can then be iced.

Prepare the icing following the instructions on page 22. Remove the cake from the freezer and pour the icing over the cake, spreading it to cover the top and sides. Leave until the icing has set.

To prepare the chantilly cream, whip the cream with the icing sugar. When it is holding its shape, spoon it into a piping bag fitted with a flat nozzle and pipe swirls backwards and forwards across the top of the cake. Dust with a little sifted cocoa powder to finish.

MATCHA MARBLE

 Serves 6-8  **Preparation time:** 25 minutes   **Cooking time:** 45 minutes

With its tricolour marbling of batters flavoured with matcha, raspberry and white chocolate, this is a very colourful cake. You can increase the amount of matcha to suit your taste, but it's worth remembering that depending on the brand and quality you use, the flavour will vary in strength.

WHITE CHOCOLATE AND MATCHA CAKE BATTERS

- 50 g (2 oz) butter, plus extra for greasing the tin and piping
- 120 g (4 oz) white chocolate
- 2 eggs
- 50 g (2 oz) caster sugar
- 100 g (3½ oz) plain flour, sifted, plus extra for dusting the tin
- 4 g (scant 1 teaspoon) baking powder
- 2 tablespoons whipping cream
- 4 g (scant 1 teaspoon) matcha green tea powder

RASPBERRY CAKE BATTER

- 15 g (½ oz) butter
- 1 egg
- 35 g (1¼ oz) caster sugar
- 55 g (2¼ oz) raspberry purée
- 55 g (2¼ oz) plain flour, sifted
- 2 g (heaped ⅓ teaspoon) baking powder
- 1 tablespoon whipping cream

To make the white chocolate and matcha cake batters, melt the butter, then leave it to cool to lukewarm. Melt the white chocolate separately.

Whisk the eggs with the sugar until thickened and fluffy, then whisk in the melted white chocolate. Fold in the sifted flour and baking powder, followed by the lukewarm butter and cream.

Divide the batter equally between 2 mixing bowls and stir the matcha powder into 1 of them.

Spoon each batter into a disposable piping bag and keep at room temperature while you prepare the raspberry cake batter.

For the raspberry cake batter, melt the butter and let it cool to lukewarm. Whisk the egg with the sugar until thickened and fluffy, then add the raspberry purée. Mix well, fold in the sifted flour and baking powder, followed by the lukewarm butter and cream. Spoon the batter into a disposable piping bag.

Preheat the oven to 160ºC (325 ºF), Gas Mark 3. Butter and flour your loaf tin.

Snip the tips off the piping bags and pipe alternate lines of the white chocolate, matcha and raspberry batters in the centre of the tin running the length of it until all 3 have been used up (see page 16). Finish by piping a line of butter down the middle of the batter (see page 16) and bake for 45 minutes.

When the cake comes out of the oven, turn it out onto a wire rack and leave it to cool.

BRILLIANTLY NUTTY

THE HAZELNUT LOVER'S CAKE	92
SICILIAN PISTACHIO	95
HAZELNUT COFFEE CAKE	96
HONEY NUT BREAKFAST CAKE	98
PECAN VANILLA	101
GLUTEN-FREE AMARETTO AND ALMOND	102
PEANUT AND CARAMEL	105

RECIPES FOR NUT LOVERS

Pistachios, pecans, almonds, pine nuts... whether as a butter, ground to a powder, whole or in praline, it's now time for nuts to step into the spotlight. Here are seven recipes featuring different nuts, either on their own or combined with honey, chocolate, vanilla or coffee. Which ones will tempt you the most?

THE HAZELNUT LOVER'S CAKE

 Serves 6–8   **Preparation time: 35 minutes**   **Cooking time: 1 hour 10 minutes**

Let's begin this new chapter with hazelnuts, which often have a starring role in my cakes. This recipe is very simple but its success will depend very much on the quality of the hazelnuts you use. My advice is to try and track down roasted hazelnuts from Piedmont, if you can, as for me they are a guarantee of the best possible quality.

CAKE BATTER

100 g (3½ oz) softened butter, plus extra for greasing the tin and piping

150 g (5 oz) plain flour, sifted, plus extra for dusting the tin

180 g (6 oz) caster sugar

75 g (3 oz) Hazelnut Butter (see page 28)

3 eggs

50 g (2 oz) ground hazelnuts

6 g (1¼ teaspoons) baking powder

2 tablespoons whipping cream

40 g (1½ oz) hazelnuts, chopped

MILK CHOCOLATE AND HAZELNUT ICING

250 g (8 oz) milk chocolate with 40% cacao

2 tablespoons plus 1 teaspoon neutral oil, such as grapeseed

50 g (2 oz) hazelnuts, finely chopped

Preheat the oven to 160ºC (325ºF), Gas Mark 3. Butter and flour your loaf tin.

To make the cake batter, beat the softened butter and sugar together, then stir in the hazelnut butter. Add the eggs, one at a time, whisking each one in before adding the next. Stir in the ground hazelnuts, the sifted flour and baking powder, then the cream and chopped hazelnuts.

Transfer the batter to the loaf tin and pipe a line of butter down the middle of the batter (see page 16). Bake the cake for 1 hour 10 minutes.

When it comes out of the oven, turn the cake out onto a wire rack and leave it to cool completely.

Make the icing following the instructions on page 22 and pour it over the cold cake. Leave until the icing has set.

SICILIAN PISTACHIO

 Serves 6–8

 **Preparation time:** 15 minutes

 Cooking time: 55 minutes

The spotlight is on Italy in this chapter. After hazelnuts from Piedmont, we have pistachios from Sicily, where that small, delicately flavoured nut is king. Pistachios go well with all types of chocolate and an attractive finish makes this cake even more indulgent.

CAKE BATTER

- 100 g (3½ oz) softened butter, plus extra for greasing the tin and piping
- 150 g (5 oz) plain flour, sifted, plus extra for dusting the tin
- 180 g (6 oz) caster sugar
- 50 g (2 oz) Pistachio Butter (see page 28)
- 3 eggs
- 70 g (2¾ oz) ground pistachios
- 6 g (1¼ teaspoons) baking powder
- 75 ml (3 fl oz) whipping cream

FOR DECORATION

- 30 g (1¼ oz) Pistachio Butter (see page 28)
- 65 g (2½ oz) pistachios, finely chopped

Preheat the oven to 160°C (325°F), Gas Mark 3. Butter and flour your loaf tin.

Beat the softened butter with the sugar and pistachio butter. When the mixture is smooth and creamy, add the eggs, one at a time, whisking each in before adding the next. Fold in the ground pistachios, followed by the sifted flour and baking powder. Finally, stir in the cream.

Transfer the batter to the loaf tin and pipe a line of butter down the middle of the batter (see page 16). Bake the cake for 55 minutes.

When the cake comes out of the oven, leave it to cool for a few minutes in the tin before turning it out onto a wire rack and leaving it to cool completely before decorating.

When the cake is cold, spread the pistachio butter over it and press the chopped pistachios on top.

HAZELNUT COFFEE CAKE

 Serves 6-8

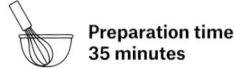 **Preparation time:** 35 minutes

 Cooking time: 50 minutes

Hazelnuts, a little coffee and a chocolate cream filling. What else could you possibly wish for? Of all the recipes in the book, this one is my favourite! As with the other cakes containing hazelnuts, I recommend you use ones from Piedmont. For this recipe, you will need a loaf tin with a cylinder insert.

CAKE BATTER

100 g (3½ oz) softened butter, plus extra for greasing the tin and piping

150 g (5 oz) plain flour, sifted, plus extra for dusting the tin

180 g (6 oz) caster sugar

50 g (2 oz) Hazelnut Butter (see page 28)

8 g (¼ oz) instant coffee granules

3 eggs

20 g (¾ oz) cold espresso

70 g (2¾ oz) ground hazelnuts

6 g (1¼ teaspoons) baking powder

75 ml (3 fl oz) whipping cream

HAZELNUT PRALINE GANACHE

40 g (1½ oz) milk chocolate with 35% cacao

40 g (1½ oz) Hazelnut Praline (see page 27)

2 tablespoons whipping cream

8 g (¼ oz) honey

12 g (½ oz) butter, diced

MILK CHOCOLATE AND HAZELNUT ICING

250 g (8 oz) milk chocolate with 40% cacao

2 tablespoons plus 1 teaspoon neutral oil, such as grapeseed

50 g (2 oz) hazelnuts, finely chopped

FOR DECORATION

1 chocolate coffee bean (optional)

Preheat the oven to 160ºC (325ºF), Gas Mark 3. Butter and flour both the loaf tin and cylinder insert, and fit the insert into the tin.

To make the cake batter, beat the softened butter with the sugar, then stir in the hazelnut butter and instant coffee granules. Add the eggs, one at a time, whisking each one in before adding the next, followed by the espresso. Fold in the ground hazelnuts, sifted flour and baking powder. Finally, stir in the cream.

Transfer the batter to the loaf tin with the insert in place and bake for 50 minutes.

When the cake comes out of the oven, leave it to cool for a few minutes before removing the insert (see page 18). Turn the cake out onto a wire rack and leave to cool completely.

While the cake is cooling, make the ganache. Melt the chocolate, then stir in the praline. Heat the cream with the honey and pour this mixture onto the chocolate and praline, stirring constantly with a spatula. When the ganache becomes smooth and shiny, add the butter, stirring until it has melted and mixed in. Leave the ganache to cool, then spoon it into a piping bag and fill the centre of the cake with it (see page 18).

Make the icing following the instructions on page 22. Pour the icing over the cake, spreading it over the top and sides (I like to pop a chocolate coffee bean on top for decoration, but it's up to you). Leave to set, then store the cake in the refrigerator until ready to serve.

HONEY NUT BREAKFAST CAKE

 Serves 6–8   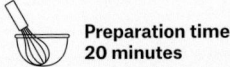 **Preparation time:** 20 minutes   **Cooking time:** 1 hour

A nut that is rarely used for making cakes, but is particularly delicious, is the pine nut. When combined with lavender honey, as in this recipe, the result is a moreish cake, perfect for serving for breakfast with cottage cheese or curd cheese.

CAKE BATTER

- 120 g (4 oz) softened butter, plus extra for greasing the tin and piping
- 180 g (6 oz) plain flour, sifted, plus extra for dusting the tin
- 60 g (2¼ oz) pine nuts
- 125 g (4 oz) lavender honey
- 50 g (2 oz) wildflower honey
- 3 eggs
- 6 g (1¼ teaspoons) baking powder
- 90 ml (3¼ fl oz) whipping cream

FOR DECORATION

- 50 g (2 oz) wildflower honey
- 45 g (1¾ oz) pine nuts

Preheat the oven to 150ºC (300ºF), Gas Mark 2. Butter and flour your loaf tin.

Spread the pine nuts over a baking sheet and roast in the oven for 15 minutes. Remove from the oven and increase the temperature to 160ºC (325ºF), Gas Mark 3.

To make the cake batter, mix the softened butter with the honeys. Beat in the eggs, one at a time, whisking each in before adding the next. Fold in the sifted flour and baking powder, followed by the cream and then the roasted pine nuts.

Transfer the batter to the loaf tin and pipe a line of butter down the middle of the batter (see page 16). Bake the cake for 1 hour.

When the cake comes out of the oven, leave it to cool in the tin for a few minutes before turning it out onto a wire rack to cool completely.

To decorate, warm the honey, then drizzle it over the cold cake. Top with the pine nuts.

PECAN VANILLA

 **Serves** 6–8

 **Preparation time:** 15 minutes

 **Cooking time:** 55 minutes

Let's head to the USA and put the popular pecan nut to the test! In this recipe, I've chosen to partner it with vanilla, which is an unbeatable combination.

CAKE BATTER

- 100 g (3½ oz) softened butter, plus extra for greasing the tin and piping
- 130 g (4¼ oz) plain flour, sifted, plus extra for dusting the tin
- 140 g (4½ oz) caster sugar
- 1 tablespoon vanilla extract
- 1 vanilla pod, split lengthways and seeds scraped out
- 4 eggs
- 120 g (4 oz) ground pecans
- 7 g (1½ teaspoons) baking powder
- 50 ml (2 fl oz) whipping cream
- 30 g (1¼ oz) pecans, chopped

Preheat the oven to 160ºC (325ºF), Gas Mark 3. Butter and flour your loaf tin.

Beat the softened butter with the sugar, then add the vanilla extract and vanilla seeds. Beat in the eggs, one at a time, whisking each in before adding the next. Fold in the ground pecans, followed by the sifted flour and baking powder. Finally, stir in the cream and the chopped pecans.

Transfer the batter to the loaf tin and pipe a line of butter down the middle of the batter (see page 16). Bake the cake for 55 minutes.

When the cake comes out of the oven, leave it to cool in the tin for a few minutes before turning it out onto a wire rack to cool completely.

GLUTEN-FREE AMARETTO AND ALMOND

 Serves 6–8 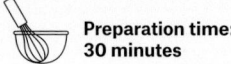 Preparation time: 30 minutes  Cooking time: 50 minutes

Now we resume our Italian adventure with amaretto, a liqueur made from bitter almonds, often used in Italian baking. When combined with ground almonds, as in this cake, it works beautifully. This cake is also gluten-free, as ground almonds replace flour.

CAKE BATTER

- a little softened butter for greasing the tin and piping
- 4 eggs
- 140 g (4½ oz) caster sugar
- 50 ml (2 fl oz) amaretto liqueur
- 150 g (5 oz) ground almonds
- 6 g (1¼ teaspoons) baking powder

BLONDE CHOCOLATE AND ALMOND ICING

- 250 g (8 oz) blonde chocolate
- 2 tablespoons neutral oil, such as grapeseed
- 50 g (2 oz) chopped almonds

To make the cake batter, preheat the oven to 160ºC (325ºF), Gas Mark 3. Grease the loaf tin with a little butter and line it with baking parchment.

Whisk the eggs with the sugar until thickened and fluffy, then whisk in the amaretto liqueur.

Mix together the ground almonds and the baking powder and fold in.

Transfer the batter to the lined tin and pipe a line of butter down the middle of the batter (see page 16). Bake the cake for 50 minutes.

When the cake comes out of the oven, turn it out onto a wire rack to cool completely.

While the cake is cooling, make the icing following the instructions on page 22. Pour the icing over the cold cake, spreading it over the top and sides, and leave to set.

PEANUT AND CARAMEL

 Serves
6–8

 Preparation time:
50 minutes

 Cooking time:
45 minutes

Inspired by the famous Snickers chocolate bar, here we have a marbled chocolate and peanut cake with a peanut caramel filling, coated in milk chocolate icing. For this recipe, you will need a loaf tin with a cylinder insert.

CAKE BATTER

50 g (2 oz) softened butter, plus extra for greasing the tin and piping

55 g (5¼ oz) plain flour, sifted, plus extra for dusting the tin

155 g (5¼ oz) caster sugar

80 g (3 oz) peanut butter

130 g (4¼ oz) eggs (2–3 large eggs)

6 g (1¼ teaspoons) baking powder

85 ml (3¼ fl oz) whipping cream

65 ml (2¼ fl oz) full-fat milk

15 g (½ oz) unsweetened cocoa powder

SOFT CARAMEL WITH PEANUTS

75 g (3 oz) caster sugar

50 ml (2 fl oz) whipping cream

25 g (1 oz) butter, diced

1 pinch of salt

40 g (1½ oz) unsalted peanuts, plus extra for decorating

MILK CHOCOLATE ICING

250 g (8 oz) milk chocolate with 40% cacao

2 tablespoons plus 1 teaspoon neutral oil, such as grapeseed

Preheat the oven to 160ºC (325ºF), Gas Mark 3. Butter and flour both your loaf tin and cylinder insert, and fit the insert into the tin (see page 18).

To make the cake batter, beat the softened butter and sugar together, then stir in the peanut butter. When the mixture is evenly combined, whisk in the eggs one at a time. Fold in the sifted flour and baking powder. Finally, stir in the cream and milk.

Divide the batter equally between 2 mixing bowls and stir the cocoa into 1 of the bowls. Spoon each batter into a disposable piping bag.

Snip the tips off the piping bags and pipe alternate lines of batters in the centre of the tin, with the insert in place, until both have been used up (see my tips on page 16). Pipe a line of butter down the middle of the batter (see page 16), then bake the cake for 45 minutes.

While the cake is baking, make the soft caramel. Prepare a dry caramel, adding the sugar a little at a time to a saucepan over a medium heat until it dissolves. At the same time, heat the cream. When the caramel is a rich amber colour, gradually pour the hot cream into it, whisking constantly. Take the saucepan off the heat and add the diced butter and the salt. Stir in the peanuts and leave the caramel to cool.

When the cake comes out of the oven, leave it for a few minutes before removing the insert (see page 18) and turning the cake out onto a wire rack to cool completely.

When the cake and the caramel are cold, spoon the caramel into a piping bag and fill the cake with it.

Make the icing following the instructions on page 22. Pour the icing over the cake, spreading it over the top and down the sides. Leave until the icing is starting to set before decorating the top of the cake with a few extra peanuts.

A TOUCH OF CITRUS

REFRESHING LIME AND BASIL	111
BLOOD ORANGE CAKE	112
LEMON MERINGUE CAKE	115
MOJITO CAKE	118
DELICIOUSLY TANGY LIME AND LEMON	121
FESTIVE CHOCOLATE ORANGE CAKE	122
CITRUS FRUIT MEDLEY	125

KNOW YOUR CITRUS FRUITS

Do you fancy a fresher-tasting cake? Well, look no further than one flavoured with citrus fruits! You could use lemon, of course, but there are many others, including lime, orange, grapefruit and kumquat, to name but a few. There are plenty to choose from and they give cakes acidity, as well as making them taste delicious. There are seven recipes in this chapter and each one is more vitamin-packed than the last.

REFRESHING LIME AND BASIL

 Serves 6–8    Preparation time: 25 minutes   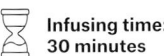 Infusing time: 30 minutes    Cooking time: 50 minutes

Basil, the aromatic herb that is the very essence of summer, is combined with lime in this cake, which lives up to its name perfectly. It certainly makes a difference from adding basil to a tomato and mozzarella salad or making pasta pesto!

CAKE BATTER

- 170 g (5¾ oz) caster sugar
- finely grated zest of 3 organic or unwaxed limes
- 8 g (¼ oz) basil leaves, finely chopped
- 50 g (2 oz) butter, plus extra for greasing the tin and piping
- 200 g (7 oz) plain flour, sifted, plus extra for dusting the tin
- 3 eggs
- 55 ml (2 fl oz) freshly squeezed lime juice
- 6 g (1¼ teaspoons) baking powder
- 50 ml (2 fl oz) whipping cream

SOAKING SYRUP

- 2 tablespoons plus 2 teaspoons freshly squeezed lime juice
- 20 g (¾ oz) icing sugar

Start by making the cake batter. Mix the sugar with the lime zest and chopped basil leaves, then leave the mixture to infuse for 30 minutes.

Melt the butter and leave it to cool to lukewarm.

Preheat the oven to 160ºC (325ºF), Gas Mark 3. Butter and flour your loaf tin.

Beat the eggs and lime juice into the infused mixture until thickened and fluffy, then fold in the sifted flour and baking powder. Stir in the lukewarm butter along with the cream.

Transfer the batter to the loaf tin and pipe a line of butter down the middle of the batter (see page 16). Bake the cake for 50 minutes.

To make the soaking syrup, mix the lime juice and icing sugar together. Brush the syrup over the cake when it comes out of the oven. Leave the cake to cool completely before turning it out.

BLOOD ORANGE CAKE

 Serves 6-8 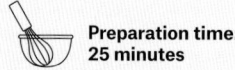 **Preparation time:** 25 minutes   **Cooking time:** 55 minutes

Orange works extremely well in baking, especially cakes. I've chosen to use blood oranges, but if you can't find them, use ordinary oranges instead. Similarly, I've made the icing with Grand Marnier, but you can use orange juice for an alcohol-free version.

CAKE BATTER

120 g (4 oz) softened butter, plus extra for greasing the tin and piping

210 g (7¼ oz) plain flour, sifted, plus extra for dusting the tin

80 g (3 oz) caster sugar

80 g (3 oz) light brown soft sugar

finely grated zest of 2 organic or unwaxed blood oranges

3 eggs

7 g (1½ teaspoons) baking powder

90 ml (3¼ fl oz) whipping cream

50 ml (2 fl oz) freshly squeezed blood orange juice

1 pinch of salt

SOAKING SYRUP

2 tablespoons blood orange juice

20 g (¾ oz) icing sugar

ICING

110 g (3¾ oz) icing sugar

2 tablespoons plus 2 teaspoons Grand Marnier (or other orange-flavoured liqueur), or see recipe introduction

Preheat the oven to 160°C (325°F), Gas Mark 3. Butter and flour your loaf tin.

To make the cake batter, beat the softened butter with the sugars and the orange zest. Beat in the eggs, one at a time, whisking each one in before adding the next. Fold in 100g (3½ oz) of the sifted flour along with the baking powder, then stir in the cream and the orange juice. Finally, fold in the remaining flour and the pinch of salt.

Transfer the batter to the loaf tin and pipe a line of butter down the middle of the batter (see page 16). Bake the cake for 55 minutes.

While the cake is baking, make the syrup by mixing the 2 ingredients together. When the cake comes out of the oven, brush the syrup over the cake and leave it to cool in the tin.

To make the icing, mix the 2 ingredients together. When the cake is cold, turn it out onto a board and pour the icing over it. Leave until the icing has set.

LEMON MERINGUE CAKE

 Serves 6–8
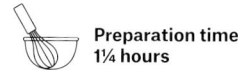 Preparation time: 1¼ hours
 Cooking time: 55 minutes

This cake is reminiscent of a classic lemon meringue pie. It can be made with different combinations of ingredients, such as lemon and hazelnut (as I've done here), lemon and almond, or even lime and hazelnut. These are just suggestions – it's up to you to discover your winning combo! For this recipe, you will need a loaf tin with a cylinder insert.

CAKE BATTER

50 g (2 oz) softened butter, plus extra for greasing the tin and piping

120 g (4 oz) plain flour, sifted, plus extra for dusting the tin

150 g (5 oz) caster sugar

finely grated zest of 2 organic or unwaxed lemons

75 g (3 oz) Hazelnut Butter (see page 28)

3 eggs

2 tablespoons plus 1 teaspoon freshly squeezed lemon juice

80 g (3 oz) ground hazelnuts

6 g (1¼ teaspoons) baking powder

50 ml (2 fl oz) whipping cream

LEMON CREAM FILLING

4 teaspoons full-fat milk

4 teaspoons whipping cream

95 ml (3½ fl oz) freshly squeezed lemon juice

1 egg

25 g (1 oz) caster sugar

15 g (½ oz) cornflour

20 g (¾ oz) butter, diced

continues overleaf >>>

Preheat the oven to 160ºC (325ºF), Gas Mark 3. Butter and flour both your loaf tin and the cylinder insert, and fit the insert into the tin (see page 18).

To make the cake batter, melt the butter and leave it to cool until lukewarm.

Mix the sugar with the lemon zest, then stir in the hazelnut butter. Beat in the eggs, one at a time, mixing each one in before adding the next. Stir in the lemon juice and ground hazelnuts, then fold in the sifted flour and baking powder. Finally, stir in the lukewarm butter followed by the cream.

Transfer the batter to the loaf tin, with the insert in place, and pipe a line of butter down the middle of the batter (see page 16). Bake the cake for 55 minutes.

While the cake is baking, make the lemon cream filling. Heat the milk with the cream and lemon juice in a saucepan. Whisk the egg with the sugar and cornflour. Whisk the hot liquid into the egg mixture, then pour it back into the saucepan. Whisk constantly over a medium heat until you have a custard that is smooth and thickened. Take the pan off the heat and add the diced butter. Mix well, until melted and homogenous, then press clingfilm over the surface of the custard and leave it in a cool place until cold. Store in the refrigerator until required.

To make the soaking syrup, mix the 2 ingredients together. When the cake comes out of the oven, brush the syrup over the cake. Leave it to cool in the tin before removing the insert and turning the cake out.

When the cake is cold, remove the lemon cream from the refrigerator and spoon it into a disposable piping bag. Snip off the tip of the bag and fill the cake with the cream (see page 18).

LEMON MERINGUE CAKE (continued)

SOAKING SYRUP

2 tablespoons freshly squeezed lemon juice

20 g (¾ oz) icing sugar

ITALIAN MERINGUE

70 g (2¾ oz) caster sugar

4 teaspoons water

35 g (1¼ oz) egg whites (from about 1 large egg)

To make the meringue, heat the sugar and water in a saucepan. When the temperature of the syrup reaches 110ºC (230ºF), begin whisking the egg whites with an electric beater. When they become mousse-like but are not stiff and the temperature of the syrup has risen to 121ºC (250ºF), pour it in a thin stream over the egg whites, whisking constantly and increasing the speed until you have a meringue that is smooth, stiff and shiny.

Spoon the meringue into a piping bag fitted with a flat nozzle and pipe it in a wavy line on top of the cake. Use a kitchen blowtorch to brown the top of the meringue, if wished.

MOJITO CAKE

 Serves 6-8 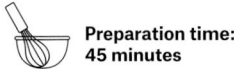 **Preparation time:** 45 minutes   **Infusing time:** 15 minutes   **Cooking time:** 55 minutes

After basil, now comes mint. Combining mint with lime and rum delivers a very aromatic mojito cake that makes the perfect dessert for a summer evening party. For an alcohol-free version, replace the rum with the same quantity of freshly squeezed lime juice.

CAKE BATTER

- 50 g (2 oz) butter, plus extra for greasing the tin and piping
- 190 g (6½ oz) light brown soft sugar
- finely grated zest of 3 organic or unwaxed limes
- 8 mint leaves, chopped
- 200 g (7 oz) plain flour, sifted, plus extra for dusting the tin
- 3 eggs
- 2 tablespoons white rum (or see recipe introduction)
- 25 ml (1 fl oz) freshly squeezed lime juice
- 6 g (1¼ teaspoons) baking powder
- 50 ml (2 fl oz) whipping cream

SOAKING SYRUP

- 4 teaspoons freshly squeezed lime juice
- 2 teaspoons white rum (or see recipe introduction)
- 20 g (¾ oz) icing sugar

ICING

- 110 g (3¾ oz) icing sugar
- 25 ml (1 fl oz) freshly squeezed lime juice
- 2 mint leaves, chopped

To make the cake batter, melt the butter and leave it to cool until lukewarm.

Mix the sugar with the lime zest and chopped mint. Leave to infuse for at least 15 minutes.

Preheat the oven to 160ºC (325ºF), Gas Mark 3. Butter and flour your loaf tin.

Whisk the eggs into the infused sugar until thickened and fluffy, followed by the rum and the lime juice. Stir in the sifted flour and baking powder, followed by the lukewarm butter and finally the cream.

Transfer the mixture to the loaf tin and pipe a line of butter down the middle of the batter (see page 16). Bake the cake for 55 minutes.

To make the soaking syrup, mix the 3 ingredients together. Brush the syrup over the cake when it comes out of the oven. Leave it to cool in the tin before turning it out.

To make the icing, mix the 3 ingredients together. When the cake is completely cold, pour the icing over it, spreading it over the top and down the sides, and leave to set at room temperature.

DELICIOUSLY TANGY LIME AND LEMON

 Serves 6-8   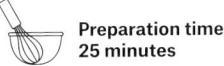 **Preparation time:** 25 minutes   **Cooking time:** 50 minutes

Lemon is certainly the most frequently used citrus fruit in baking. For fans of a citrussy tang, this recipe provides a double hit as it includes both lemon and lime.

CAKE BATTER

- 50 g (2 oz) butter, plus extra for greasing the tin and piping
- 200 g (7 oz) plain flour, sifted, plus extra for dusting the tin
- 170 g (5¾ oz) caster sugar
- finely grated zest of 1 organic or unwaxed lemon
- finely grated zest of 1 organic or unwaxed lime
- 3 eggs
- 2 tablespoons freshly squeezed lemon juice
- 1 tablespoon plus 2 teaspoons freshly squeezed lime juice
- 6 g (1¼ teaspoons) baking powder
- 50 ml (2 fl oz) whipping cream

SOAKING SYRUP

- 20 g (¾ oz) icing sugar
- 1 tablespoon freshly squeezed lime juice
- 1 tablespoon freshly squeezed lemon juice

FOR DECORATION (OPTIONAL)

- 1 lemon and/or lime, sliced

Preheat the oven to 160ºC (325ºF), Gas Mark 3. Butter and flour your loaf tin.

To make the cake batter, melt the butter, then leave it to cool until lukewarm.

Whisk the sugar with the citrus zests, then add the eggs, citrus juices, sifted flour and baking powder, the lukewarm butter and the cream, in that order, whisking constantly.

Transfer the batter to the loaf tin and pipe a line of butter down the middle of the batter (see page 16). Bake the cake for 50 minutes.

To make the syrup, mix the icing sugar with the citrus juices. Brush the syrup over the cake when it comes out of the oven and leave it to cool in the tin before turning it out. Decorate with lime and lemon slices, if you like.

FESTIVE CHOCOLATE ORANGE CAKE

 Serves 6-8

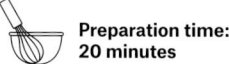 **Preparation time:** 20 minutes

 **Cooking time:** 55 minutes

Covered with dark chocolate icing, this chocolate, cocoa and orange cake, studded with pieces of candied orange peel, will remind you of chocolate-coated orangettes, the sweet treat that often appears in the shops around Christmastime. If you want to try something a little different from the original, this cake is equally tasty when made with clementine or even grated zest and candied lemon peel.

CAKE BATTER

100 g (3½ oz) softened butter, plus extra for greasing the tin and piping

150 g (5 oz) plain flour, sifted, plus extra for dusting the tin

150 g (5 oz) dark chocolate with 70% cacao, chopped

140 g (4½ oz) caster sugar

finely grated zest of 1 organic or unwaxed orange

3 eggs

50 ml (2 fl oz) orange juice

25 g (1 oz) unsweetened cocoa powder

6 g (1¼ teaspoons) baking powder

55 ml (2 fl oz) whipping cream

40 g (1½ oz) candied orange peel, finely chopped, plus extra pieces for decoration

SOAKING SYRUP

2 tablespoons plus 1 teaspoon orange juice

20 g (¾ oz) icing sugar

DARK CHOCOLATE ICING

250 g (8 oz) dark chocolate with 66% cacao

3 tablespoons neutral oil, such as grapeseed

Preheat the oven to 160ºC (325ºF), Gas Mark 3. Butter and flour your loaf tin.

To make the cake batter, melt the chocolate in a bain-marie. Allow to cool slightly.

Beat the softened butter with the sugar and the orange zest. Add the eggs, one at a time, whisking each one in before adding the next, then whisk in the orange juice.

Stir in the melted chocolate, followed by the sifted flour, cocoa and baking powder. Finally, stir in the cream and chopped candied orange peel.

Transfer the batter to the loaf tin and pipe a line of butter down the middle of the batter (see page 16). Bake the cake for 55 minutes.

While the cake is baking, make the soaking syrup by mixing the 2 ingredients together. When the cake comes out of the oven, brush the syrup over it. Leave the cake to cool in the tin before turning it out.

Make the icing following the instructions on page 22. Pour the icing over the cake, spreading it over the top and down the sides. Decorate the top with pieces of candied orange peel and leave until the icing has set.

CITRUS FRUIT MEDLEY

 Serves 6-8

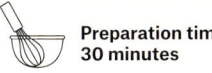 **Preparation time:** 30 minutes

 Cooking time: 55 minutes

What better way to start your day? A cake that's guaranteed to get you going, thanks to all the citrus fruits it contains!

CAKE BATTER

100 g (3½ oz) butter, plus extra for greasing the tin and piping

210 g (7¼ oz) plain flour, sifted, plus extra for dusting the tin

3 eggs

150 g (5 oz) caster sugar

finely grated zests of 1 citron (or regular lemon), 1 clementine, 1 makrut lime (or regular lime) and 1 grapefruit

1 kumquat, finely chopped

2 teaspoons freshly squeezed citron (or lemon) juice

4 teaspoons freshly squeezed clementine juice

4 teaspoons freshly squeezed grapefruit juice

6 g (1¼ teaspoons) baking powder

90 ml (3¼ fl oz) whipping cream

SOAKING SYRUP

20 g (¾ oz) icing sugar

2 teaspoons freshly squeezed grapefruit juice

2 teaspoons freshly squeezed citron (or lemon) juice

2 teaspoons freshly squeezed clementine juice

CITRUS FRUIT ICING

90 g (3¼ oz) icing sugar

2 teaspoons freshly squeezed grapefruit juice

2 teaspoons freshly squeezed citron (or lemon) juice

2 teaspoons freshly squeezed clementine juice

Preheat the oven to 160ºC (325ºF), Gas Mark 3. Butter and flour your loaf tin.

To make the cake batter, melt the butter and leave it to cool to lukewarm.

Whisk the eggs with the sugar until thickened and fluffy, then add the citrus zests and finely chopped kumquat. Whisk in the citrus juices, followed by the sifted flour and baking powder. Finally, add the lukewarm butter and cream, whisking between each addition.

Transfer the mixture to the loaf tin and pipe a line of butter down the middle of the batter (see page 16). Bake the cake for 55 minutes.

To make the syrup, mix the icing sugar and citrus juices together. When the cake comes out of the oven, pour the syrup over it, letting it run down into the tin. Leave the cake to cool completely before turning it out.

To make the icing, mix the icing sugar and citrus juices together. Stand the cold cake on a wire rack and pour the icing over it, spreading it over the top and down the sides. Leave until the icing has set.

A TRIP TO THE MARKET

NORMANDY APPLE AND CARAMEL 130

CHOCOLATE AND COCONUT CAKE 132

PUMPKIN SPICE 135

SEASONAL FRUITS YOUR WAY 136

BANANA, CHOCOLATE AND PEANUT CAKE 138

PERFECTLY SPICED CARROT CAKE 141

UNPACKING YOUR BASKET

Chopped apple, puréed squash, grated carrots... When making a cake, the fruit and vegetable world is your oyster! Citrus fruits have already been celebrated with their own dedicated chapter in this book, but other fruits and even some vegetables can be used to make mouthwatering cakes. Take, for example, the very popular carrot cake or the American pumpkin spice cake with cream cheese frostings. When it comes to cakes made with fresh fruit, I love the classic banana and chocolate cake, but apples and berries will also produce stunning results.

NORMANDY APPLE AND CARAMEL

 Serves 6–8   **Preparation time:** 1 hour   **Cooking time:** 1 hour 20 minutes

Are you looking for a special occasion cake or Sunday lunch dessert? One that (almost) everyone will enjoy? If so, you are on the right page. This cake with apples, caramel and whipped vanilla cream simply melts in the mouth! For this recipe, you will need a loaf tin with a cylinder insert.

CAKE BATTER

- 215 g (7¼ oz) caster sugar
- 60 ml (2¼ fl oz) whipping cream
- 1 medium apple, peeled, cored and cut into 1 cm (½ inch) cubes (about 120 g/4 oz prepared weight)
- 130 g (4¼ oz) softened butter, plus extra for greasing the tin and piping
- 180 g (6 oz) plain flour, sifted, plus extra for dusting the tin
- 1 teaspoon vanilla extract
- 3 eggs
- 7 g (1½ teaspoons) baking powder

CHANTILLY CREAM

- 160 g (5½ oz) double or whipping cream
- 75 g (3 oz) mascarpone
- 25 g (1 oz) icing sugar
- 1 vanilla pod, split lengthways and seeds scraped out

FILLING

- 30 g (1¼ oz) caster sugar
- 25 ml (1 fl oz) whipping cream
- 1 small apple, peeled and cored and cut into 5 mm (¼ inch) cubes (about 90 g/3¼ oz prepared weight)

To make the cake batter, prepare a dry caramel by gradually adding 75 g (3 oz) of the sugar to a saucepan over a medium heat until it melts. At the same time, heat the whipping cream in a separate saucepan. When the caramel is a rich amber colour, deglaze the pan by whisking in the cream. Spoon out 1–2 tablespoons of the caramel into a bowl and set aside for decorating the cake later. Add the apple cubes to the pan and stir well until coated in the caramel. Leave them to cook over a low heat for 10 minutes, then remove the pan from the heat and leave the mixture to cool.

Preheat the oven to 160ºC (325ºF), Gas Mark 3. Butter and flour both the loaf tin and cylinder insert, and fit the insert into the tin (see page 18).

Beat the softened butter with the remaining sugar and the vanilla. Beat in the eggs, one at a time, mixing each one in before adding the next, then fold in the sifted flour and baking powder. Finally, add the caramelized apple.

Transfer the mixture to the loaf tin and pipe a line of butter down the middle of the batter (see page 16). Bake the cake for 55 minutes.

While the cake is baking, make the chantilly cream. Mix all the ingredients together, then whip until the cream is holding its shape. Spoon 80 g (3 oz) of the cream into a separate bowl and put the rest into a piping bag fitted with a plain 18 mm (¾ inch) nozzle. Chill both the bowl and the piping bag in the refrigerator until needed.

When the cake comes out of the oven, leave it to cool in the tin for a few minutes, before removing the insert (see page 18) and turning the cake out onto a wire rack. Leave it to cool completely at room temperature.

To make the filling, prepare a dry caramel with the sugar in a saucepan over a medium heat. At the same time, heat the whipping cream. When the caramel is ready, deglaze the pan with the hot cream, then add the apple cubes. Leave them to cook over a low heat for 15 minutes until the apple cubes are very soft and caramelized. Remove the pan from the heat.

When the caramelized apples are cold, fold them into the bowl of whipped cream and transfer to a piping bag. Fill the cake with the mixture (see page 18).

Pipe the plain chantilly cream on top of the cake to decorate and spoon a few pools of the reserved caramel on top to finish.

CHOCOLATE AND COCONUT CAKE

 Serves 6–8  **Preparation time:** 35 minutes   **Cooking time:** 1¼ hours

Another recipe inspired by a chocolate bar, this time the chocolate-covered coconut Bounty, which is popular in France and the UK. This makes a luxurious cake with coconut and milk chocolate.

CAKE BATTER

75 g (3 oz) softened butter, plus extra for greasing the tin and piping

115 g (3¾ oz) plain flour, sifted, plus extra for dusting the tin

140 g (4½ oz) caster sugar

3 eggs

⅔ teaspoon salt

130 g (4¼ oz) coconut milk powder (source online, or from a health food shop)

6 g (1¼ teaspoons) baking powder

125 g (4 oz) coconut cream

140 g (4½ oz) milk chocolate chips

MILK CHOCOLATE ICING

250 g (8 oz) milk chocolate with 40% cacao

2 tablespoons plus 1 teaspoon neutral oil, such as grapeseed

FOR DECORATION

2 tablespoons desiccated coconut

coconut flakes, for sprinkling

Preheat the oven to 160ºC (325ºF), Gas Mark 3. Butter and flour your loaf tin.

To make the cake batter, beat the softened butter with the sugar. Beat in the eggs, one at a time, whisking each one in before adding the next, then stir in the salt, coconut milk powder and the sifted flour and baking powder. When the batter is smooth, add the coconut cream and the milk chocolate chips.

Transfer the mixture to the loaf tin and pipe a line of butter down the middle of the batter (see page 16). Bake the cake for 1¼ hours.

When the cake comes out of the oven, leave it to cool in the tin for a few minutes before turning it out onto a wire rack to cool completely.

Make the icing following the instructions on page 22. Pour the icing over the cold cake, spreading it over the top and down the sides. Dust with the desiccated coconut, add a sprinkling of coconut flakes and leave until the icing has set.

PUMPKIN SPICE

 Serves 6–8

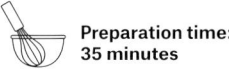 **Preparation time:** 35 minutes

 Cooking time: 45 minutes

After the fruits, here come the vegetables! In this cake, pumpkin takes pride of place in a recipe that's hugely popular in the United States: pumpkin spice cake. With its rich cream-cheese frosting, it makes an ideal autumn teatime treat.

CAKE BATTER

110 g (3¾ oz) softened butter, plus extra for greasing the tin and piping

175 g (6 oz) plain flour, sifted, plus extra for dusting the tin

210 g (7¼ oz) pumpkin purée

75 ml (3 fl oz) full-fat milk

1 teaspoon vanilla extract

1 tablespoon ground cinnamon

1 teaspoon ground ginger

1 teaspoon freshly grated nutmeg

1 pinch of ground cloves

1 pinch of salt

130 g (4¼ oz) caster sugar

2 eggs

6 g (1¼ teaspoons) baking powder

FROSTING

90 g (3¼ oz) cream cheese (such as Philadelphia)

1 teaspoon vanilla extract

45 g (1¾ oz) icing sugar

Preheat the oven to 175°C (345°F), Gas Mark 3½. Butter and flour your loaf tin.

To make the cake batter, mix together the pumpkin purée, milk, vanilla, spices and salt.

In a separate mixing bowl, beat the butter with the sugar, then beat in the eggs, one at a time, whisking each one in before adding the next.

Fold in 75 g (3 oz) of the flour, sifted with the baking powder, then stir in the pumpkin mixture. Finally, sift in the remaining flour and fold it in.

Transfer the batter to the loaf tin and pipe a line of butter down the middle of the batter (see page 16). Bake the cake for 45 minutes.

When the cake comes out of the oven, turn it out onto a wire rack and leave it to cool completely.

To make the frosting, stir together the cream cheese, vanilla and icing sugar until combined. When the cake is cold, spread the icing over it using a spatula and store in the refrigerator until ready to serve.

SEASONAL FRUITS YOUR WAY

 Serves 6–8

 **Preparation time:** 40 minutes

 Cooking time: 1 hour

You can adapt this cake recipe by using some of your favourite fruit flavours. From raspberry, passion fruit and pear to apple and red berry fruits, the choice is yours. Have fun with the icings for decorating your cake, such as dark chocolate and almond icing for a pear cake, milk chocolate for one made with passion fruit, or even a blonde chocolate and almond icing for a raspberry-flavoured cake.

CAKE BATTER

60 g (2¼ oz) butter, plus extra for greasing the tin and piping

200 g (7 oz) plain flour, sifted, plus extra for dusting the tin

4 eggs

120 g (4 oz) caster sugar

200 g (7 oz) fruit purée of your choice (see recipe introduction)

50 ml (2 fl oz) whipping cream

7 g (1½ teaspoons) baking powder

SOAKING SYRUP

1 tablespoon fruit purée

4 teaspoons water

2 teaspoons caster sugar

ICING OF YOUR CHOICE

(optional; see pages 22–26 and recipe introduction)

Preheat the oven to 160ºC (325ºF), Gas Mark 3. Butter and flour your loaf tin.

To make the cake batter, melt the butter and leave it to cool until lukewarm.

Whisk the eggs with the sugar until thickened and fluffy, then add your fruit purée along with the whipping cream.

Fold in the sifted flour and baking powder, then finally the lukewarm butter.

Transfer the mixture to the loaf tin and pipe a line of butter down the middle of the batter (see page 16). Bake the cake for 1 hour.

To make the syrup, bring the 3 ingredients to the boil in a saucepan. When the sugar has dissolved completely, remove the pan from the heat. When the cake comes out of the oven, brush the syrup over it, then leave it to cool in the tin.

Choose your icing, if you want it. When your icing is ready, place the cake on a wire rack and pour the icing over it. Leave until the icing has set.

BANANA, CHOCOLATE AND PEANUT CAKE

 **Serves** 6–8　　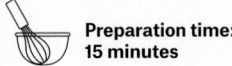 **Preparation time:** 15 minutes　　 **Cooking time:** 1 hour 5 minutes

If you want a combination of ingredients that works every time, look no further than banana, chocolate and peanut. To ring the changes, replace the peanut butter with hazelnut or almond butter and the dark chocolate with milk chocolate (but remember to reduce the quantity of sugar you add, as milk chocolate is sweeter). These might be subtle variations, but the results are always delicious.

CAKE BATTER

- a little butter for greasing the tin and piping
- 115 g (3¾ oz) plain flour, sifted, plus extra for dusting the tin
- 80 g (3 oz) dark chocolate with 66% cacao, chopped
- 300 g (10 oz) very ripe bananas (peeled weight)
- 70 g (2¾ oz) light brown soft sugar
- 80 g (3 oz) peanut butter
- 2 large eggs (weighing 115 g/3¾ oz without the shells)
- 80 g (3 oz) ground almonds
- 40 g (1½ oz) unsweetened cocoa powder
- 7 g (1½ teaspoons) baking powder

FOR DECORATION

- ½ banana, split lengthways (optional)
- a few peanuts, halved (optional)

Preheat the oven to 160ºC (325ºF), Gas Mark 3. Butter and flour your loaf tin.

Gently melt the chocolate in a bain-marie. Allow to cool slightly.

Mash the bananas, then mix them first with the sugar, followed by the peanut butter and then the eggs. Whisk the mixture until smooth, then add the melted chocolate. Fold in the ground almonds, followed by the flour, sifted with the cocoa and baking powder.

Transfer the mixture to the loaf tin and pipe a line of butter down the middle of the batter (see page 16). If using, press the banana half and a few peanuts into the top of the batter for decoration. Bake the cake for 1 hour 5 minutes.

When the cake comes out of the oven, leave it to cool in the tin for a few minutes before turning it out onto a wire rack to cool completely.

PERFECTLY SPICED CARROT CAKE

 Serves 6–8

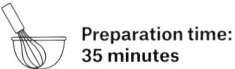 **Preparation time:** 35 minutes

 Cooking time: 1 hour

Let's end this chapter on fruits and vegetables from your local market with another popular cake – the carrot cake. Topped with a cream cheese frosting and packed with nuts, spices, vanilla and, of course, carrots, it's a cake with a deliciously moist, melt-in-the-mouth texture. It's the perfect way to eat vegetables!

CAKE BATTER

- a little butter for greasing the tin
- 130 g (4¼ oz) plain flour, sifted, plus extra for dusting the tin
- 160 ml (5½ fl oz) neutral oil, such as grapeseed
- 95 g (3¼ oz) caster sugar
- 80 g (3 oz) muscovado sugar
- 3 eggs
- 1 tablespoon vanilla extract
- 6 g (1¼ teaspoons) baking powder
- 50 g (2 oz) ground hazelnuts
- 1 tablespoon ground cinnamon
- ½ teaspoon freshly grated nutmeg
- ½ teaspoon ground cloves
- 230 g (7½ oz) grated carrots
- 50 g (2 oz) chopped nuts (walnuts, hazelnuts, almonds or pecans), plus extra for decoration

FROSTING

- 35 g (1¼ oz) softened butter
- 80 g (3 oz) icing sugar
- 165 g (5½ oz) cream cheese (such as Philadelphia)
- 1 tablespoon vanilla extract

Preheat the oven to 180°C (350°F), Gas Mark 4. Butter and flour your loaf tin.

To make the cake batter, mix the oil with the sugars, then add the eggs, vanilla extract and sifted flour and baking powder. Stir in the ground hazelnuts, spices and grated carrots. Finally, add the chopped nuts.

Transfer the batter to the loaf tin and bake for 1 hour.

When the cake comes out of the oven, leave it to cool in the tin for a few minutes before turning it out onto a wire rack to cool to room temperature.

Meanwhile, make the frosting. Beat the butter with the icing sugar. Once the mixture is smooth and creamy, stir in the cream cheese and the vanilla extract.

Once the cake is cold, cut it in half and sandwich with some of the frosting. Using a spatula, spread the rest of the frosting over the top of the cake. Decorate with a few chopped nuts and chill in the refrigerator until ready to serve.

PÂTISSERIE FAVOURITES

TIRAMISU CAKE 146

CREAMY CHEESECAKE LOAF 149

CRÈME BRÛLÉE 150

CHOCOLATE CHIP COOKIE CAKE 152

HAZELNUT FINANCIER 154

GIANT MADELEINE 157

PARIS-BREST CAKE 158

STEP INTO THE CAKE SHOP

This chapter is dedicated to cakes inspired by popular gâteaux and desserts. You will find Paris-Brest, cheesecake, tiramisu and even vanilla crème brûlée, all made in the shape of a loaf cake! Other delights are also given a new look, such as the famous madeleine, the financier and the classic chocolate chip cookie. The only hard part will be deciding which one to make first...

TIRAMISU CAKE

 Serves 6-8  **Preparation time:** 30 minutes   **Cooking time:** 1 hour

This is an extremely popular dessert, not just in Italy where it originated, but also around the world. Here, I have imagined its alter ego, a tiramisu loaf cake. Made with mascarpone and coffee with a touch of cocoa, it is filled and topped with a mascarpone cream lightly flavoured with coffee. Of course, I've given it a final dusting of cocoa powder for that characteristic tiramisu flourish. For this recipe, you will need a loaf tin with a cylinder insert.

CAKE BATTER

- a little butter for greasing the tin and piping
- 200 g (7 oz) plain flour, sifted, plus extra for dusting the tin
- 4 eggs
- 180 g (6 oz) caster sugar
- 15 g (½ oz) instant coffee
- 250 g (8 oz) mascarpone
- 15 g (½ oz) unsweetened cocoa powder, plus extra for decoration
- 6 g (1¼ teaspoons) baking powder
- 25 ml (1 fl oz) whipping cream

COFFEE-FLAVOURED MASCARPONE CREAM

- 175 ml (6 fl oz) whipping cream
- 75 g (3 oz) mascarpone
- 25 g (1 oz) icing sugar
- 5 g (2 heaped teaspoons) instant coffee

Preheat the oven to 160°C (325°F), Gas Mark 3. Butter and flour both your loaf tin and the cylinder insert, and fit the insert into the tin (see page 18).

To make the cake batter, whisk the eggs with the sugar and instant coffee until thickened and fluffy, then add the mascarpone. Fold in the sifted flour, cocoa powder and baking powder and finally stir in the cream, mixing well.

Transfer the batter to the loaf tin with the insert in place and pipe a line of butter down the middle of the batter (see page 16). Bake the cake for 1 hour.

When the cake comes out of the oven, leave it to stand in the tin for a few minutes before removing the insert (see page 18). Turn the cake out onto a wire rack and leave to cool.

To make the coffee-flavoured mascarpone cream, whip all the ingredients together until the cream is holding its shape.

When the cake is completely cold, fill the centre with some of the cream (see page 18). Spoon the remaining cream into a piping bag fitted with a flat nozzle and pipe it in a wavy line on top of the cake. Finish by lightly dusting the piped cream with cocoa powder.

CREAMY CHEESECAKE LOAF

 **Serves** 6-8  **Preparation time:** 30 minutes  **Cooking time:** 2 hours 10 minutes **Chill time:** overnight

Fans of cheesecake are guaranteed to love this luscious, creamy cake. Serve with a tangy raspberry coulis.

BISCUIT BASE

- 60 g (2¼ oz) softened butter
- 30 g (1¼ oz) light brown soft sugar
- 20 g (¾ oz) ground almonds
- 15 g (½ oz) beaten egg (about ¼ medium egg)
- 35 g (1¼ oz) plain flour, sifted

CREAM CHEESE TOPPING

- 210 g (7¼ oz) cream cheese (such as Philadelphia)
- 75 g (3 oz) caster sugar
- 20 g (¾ oz) plain flour, sifted
- 280 g (9 oz) Greek yogurt
- 100 ml (3½ fl oz) whipping cream
- 2 eggs

Preheat the oven to 170°C (345°F), Gas Mark 3½.

To make the base, beat 40 g (1½ oz) of the softened butter with 20 g (¾ oz) of the brown sugar. Stir in the ground almonds, followed by the egg and the flour. Mix to make a soft dough, then roll the dough out to 3 mm (⅛ inch) thick between 2 sheets of baking parchment. Bake in the oven for 15 minutes until golden brown.

Remove the base from the oven and leave to cool, then transfer to a food processor and blitz it into crumbs. Mix the crumbs with the remaining softened butter and brown sugar.

Line your loaf tin with baking parchment, then press the biscuit mixture over the base and lower sides of the tin, pressing it down firmly in an even layer with the back of a spoon.

Preheat the oven to 150°C (300°F), Gas Mark 2.

To make the cream cheese topping, mix the cream cheese with the sugar, then add the flour. Thoroughly mix in the yogurt, followed by the cream and finally the eggs. Pour or spoon the mixture over the biscuit base.

Bake for 20 minutes, then reduce the oven temperature to 140°C (275°F), Gas Mark 1 and bake for a further 1 hour.

At the end of the cooking time, switch off the oven and leave the cheesecake inside to cool, with the oven door open for the first 5 minutes and then closed for 30 minutes. After that time, remove the cheesecake from the oven and leave it to cool completely at room temperature before chilling it overnight in the refrigerator.

The next day, turn the cheesecake out and serve it with a fruit coulis and fresh fruit, or some caramel sauce.

CRÈME BRÛLÉE

 **Serves** 6–8

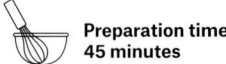 **Preparation time:** 45 minutes

 **Cooking time:** 55 minutes

We are continuing our tour of favourite desserts with this variation of crème brûlée, which I've baked as a vanilla and caramel loaf cake. Filled with vanilla mousseline to represent the creamy custard base, it is topped with caramel to add the dessert's characteristic crunchy topping. For this recipe, you will need a loaf tin with a cylinder insert.

CAKE BATTER

- 105 g (3½ oz) softened butter, plus extra for greasing the tin and piping
- 250 g (8 oz) plain flour, sifted, plus extra for dusting the tin
- 105 g (3½ oz) caster sugar
- 105 ml (3½ fl oz) whipping cream
- 120 g (4 oz) light brown soft sugar
- 1 vanilla pod, split lengthways and seeds scraped out
- 4 eggs
- 6 g (1¼ teaspoons) baking powder

VANILLA MOUSSELINE CREAM

- 3 tablespoons milk
- 2 tablespoons plus 2 teaspoons whipping cream
- 1 vanilla pod, split lengthways and seeds scraped out
- 20 g (¾ oz) egg yolk (about 1)
- 20 g (¾ oz) caster sugar
- 8 g (¼ oz) cornflour
- 60 g (2¼ oz) softened butter

CARAMEL

- 150 g (5 oz) caster sugar

Preheat the oven to 160ºC (325ºF), Gas Mark 3. Butter and flour both your loaf tin and the cylinder insert, and fit the insert into the tin (see page 18).

To make the cake batter, prepare a dry caramel by adding the caster sugar a little at a time to a saucepan set over a medium heat until the sugar has dissolved and becomes a rich amber colour. At the same time, heat the cream in a separate pan. Deglaze the caramel by gradually pouring the cream into it in a thin, steady stream, whisking constantly. Take the pan off the heat and leave the caramel to cool.

Beat the softened butter with the brown sugar and vanilla seeds, then add the eggs, one at a time, whisking constantly. Pour in the caramel and mix in, then fold in the sifted flour and baking powder.

Transfer the mixture to the loaf tin with the insert in place and pipe a line of butter down the middle of the batter (see page 16). Bake the cake for 55 minutes.

When the cake comes out of the oven, leave it to stand in the tin for a few minutes before removing the insert (see page 18). Turn out the cake onto a wire rack and leave it to cool.

To make the mousseline cream, heat the milk with the cream and vanilla seeds in a saucepan. Whisk the egg yolk with the sugar and cornflour in a heatproof mixing bowl, then pour the hot cream over it, whisking constantly. Return the mixture to the saucepan and whisk it constantly over a low heat until you have a smooth, thickened custard. Take the pan off the heat, stir in 10 g (½ oz) of the butter and pour into a clean mixing bowl. Press clingfilm over the surface and leave the custard to cool.

When it has cooled to room temperature, dice the remaining butter and whisk it gradually into the custard. Continue whisking for a few minutes until you have a smooth, mousse-like cream. If the cream splits, use a kitchen blowtorch to warm the outside of the bowl or warm the bowl for a few seconds in hot water and continue to whisk until the cream is smooth.

Spoon the cream into a piping bag and fill the cold cake with it (see page 18).

For the caramel to finish, prepare a dry caramel by adding the caster sugar a little at a time to a saucepan set over a medium heat until the sugar has dissolved and becomes a rich amber colour, then immediately drizzle over the cake. Leave the caramel to set, then store the cake in the refrigerator.

CHOCOLATE CHIP COOKIE CAKE

 Serves 6–8    **Preparation time:** 20 minutes   **Cooking time:** 50 minutes

A cake that's like a cookie naturally has to mean plenty of chocolate chips! This one has a soft, crumbly texture, is lightly flavoured with vanilla and sprinkled with hazelnuts. Let me give you a quick tip: put the chocolate chips and chopped hazelnuts in the freezer while you make the batter, to stop them sinking to the bottom of the tin during baking. You can replace the hazelnuts with another nut of your choice and add milk chocolate chips instead of dark, or even a mixture of the two.

CAKE BATTER

- 130 g (4¼ oz) softened butter, plus extra for greasing the tin and piping
- 260 g (8½ oz) plain flour, sifted, plus extra for dusting the tin
- 160 g (5½ oz) light brown soft sugar
- 2 tablespoons vanilla extract
- 3 eggs
- 6 g (1¼ teaspoons) baking powder
- 150 g (5 oz) dark chocolate chips
- 70 g (2¾ oz) chopped hazelnuts

Preheat the oven to 200ºC (400ºF), Gas Mark 6. Butter and flour your loaf tin.

Beat the softened butter with the brown sugar and vanilla extract. Beat in the eggs, one at a time, mixing each one in before adding the next, then stir in the sifted flour and baking powder followed by the chocolate chips and finally the chopped hazelnuts.

Transfer the batter to the loaf tin and pipe a line of butter down the middle of the batter (see page 16). Put the cake in the oven and immediately reduce the temperature to 170ºC (345ºF), Gas Mark 3½. Bake the cake for 50 minutes.

As soon as the cake comes out of the oven, leave it to cool in the tin for a few minutes before turning it out onto a wire rack to cool completely.

HAZELNUT FINANCIER

 Serves 6-8 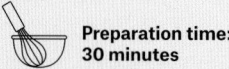 **Preparation time:** 30 minutes   **Cooking time:** 50 minutes

This cake is like a hazelnut financier filled and frosted with chocolate ganache. The inspiration for it is the famous little 'tigré' cake, created more than twenty-five years ago by Frédéric Bau at Valrhona chocolate, which has since gained in popularity mainly thanks to top French chef Cyril Lignac. For this recipe, you will need a loaf tin with a cylinder insert.

CAKE BATTER

200 g (7 oz) butter, plus extra for greasing the tin

65 g (2½ oz) plain flour, sifted, plus extra for dusting the tin

200 g (7 oz) egg whites

220 g (7½ oz) icing sugar

140 g (4½ oz) ground hazelnuts

80 g (3 oz) chocolate vermicelli

CHOCOLATE GANACHE

130 g (4¼ oz) dark chocolate with 66% cacao, chopped

150 ml (5 fl oz) whipping cream

2 tablespoons neutral-flavoured honey

30 g (1¼ oz) butter, cut into small pieces

FOR DECORATION

1 pinch of granulated sugar

Preheat the oven to 180°C (350°F), Gas Mark 4. Butter and flour both your loaf tin and the cylinder insert, and fit the insert into the tin (see page 18).

To make the cake batter, first prepare a brown butter. Cut the butter into small pieces, place it in a saucepan and leave it over a low heat to melt. Continue to cook the butter until it stops spitting and has turned a rich amber colour. Remove the pan from the heat, tip into a bowl and leave the butter to cool.

Whisk the egg whites with the icing sugar and ground hazelnuts until thickened and fluffy. Fold in the sifted flour, followed by the cooled brown butter. Finally, stir in the chocolate vermicelli.

Transfer the batter to the loaf tin with the insert in place. Bake the cake for 50 minutes.

When the cake comes out of the oven, leave it to stand in the tin for a few minutes before removing the insert (see page 18). Turn out the cake onto a wire rack and leave to cool completely.

Meanwhile, make the chocolate ganache. Melt the chocolate. At the same time, heat the cream with the honey in a saucepan. Pour the hot cream in 3 equal amounts onto the melted chocolate, stirring with a spatula until you have a shiny, smooth ganache. Gradually stir in the butter, then leave the ganache to cool.

When the texture of the ganache is mousse-like, spoon some of it into a piping bag and use it to fill the cake (see page 18). Spread the rest of the ganache over the cake using a spatula. Serve the cake sprinkled with a little granulated sugar on top.

GIANT MADELEINE

 Serves 6–8   **Preparation time:** 20 minutes   **Resting time:** overnight   **Cooking time:** 1 hour 10 minutes

Do you fancy an XXL madeleine? If so, here is a recipe for one in loaf cake form. I've flavoured it with orange and chocolate, but you can add whatever aromatics you wish, such as vanilla, tonka bean, lemon, cinnamon or orange flower water.

CAKE BATTER

- 190 g (6½ oz) butter, plus extra for greasing the tin and piping
- 3 eggs
- 120 g (4 oz) caster sugar
- finely grated zest of 1 orange, plus a little extra for decoration
- 2 tablespoons plus 2 teaspoons full-fat milk
- 170 g (5¾ oz) plain flour, sifted, plus extra for dusting the tin
- 4 g (scant 1 teaspoon) baking powder
- 60 g (2¼ oz) dark chocolate with 66% cacao, finely chopped

ICING

- 120 g (4 oz) icing sugar
- 4 teaspoons freshly squeezed orange juice

Begin making the cake batter the day before. Melt the butter and leave it to cool to lukewarm.

Whisk the eggs with the sugar and orange zest until thickened and fluffy, then whisk in the milk. Fold in the sifted flour and baking powder, then stir in the lukewarm butter and finally the chopped chocolate. Press clingfilm over the surface of the batter and let it rest in the refrigerator overnight.

The next day, preheat the oven to 220ºC (425ºF), Gas Mark 7. Butter and flour your loaf tin.

Transfer the rested batter to the loaf tin and pipe a line of butter down the middle of the batter (see page 16). Put the cake in the oven, reduce the temperature to 170ºC (345ºF), Gas Mark 3½ and bake the cake for 1 hour 10 minutes.

When the cake comes out of the oven, turn it out onto a wire rack and leave it to cool.

When the cake is cold, make the icing. Mix together the icing sugar and orange juice, then pour the icing over the cake, letting it run down the sides. Decorate with a little extra orange zest. Leave the icing to set before serving.

PARIS-BREST CAKE

 Serves 6-8

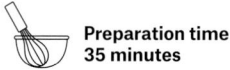 **Preparation time:** 35 minutes

 Cooking time: 1 hour

We're now off to Brittany for one of the most indulgent cakes there is, the Paris-Brest of course! Everyone knows this crown of choux pastry filled with mousseline cream and, in this recipe, I've transformed it into a hazelnut cake filled with an irresistible praline cream. For this recipe, you will need a loaf tin with a cylinder insert.

CAKE BATTER

100 g (3 ½ oz) softened butter, plus extra for greasing the tin and piping

150 g (5 oz) plain flour, sifted, plus extra for dusting the tin

150 g (5 oz) caster sugar

70 g (2¾ oz) Hazelnut Praline (see page 27)

3 eggs

70 g (2¾ oz) ground hazelnuts

6 g (1¼ teaspoons) baking powder

75 ml (3 fl oz) whipping cream

PRALINE CREAM

150 ml (5 fl oz) whipping cream, well-chilled

75 g (3 oz) mascarpone

15 g (½ oz) icing sugar

130 g (4¼ oz) Hazelnut Praline (see page 27)

FOR DECORATION

10 g (½ oz) hazelnuts, finely chopped

Preheat the oven to 160ºC (325ºF), Gas Mark 3. Butter and flour both your loaf tin and the cylinder insert, and fit the insert into the tin (see page 18).

To make the cake batter, beat the softened butter with the caster sugar. When the mixture is smooth and creamy, stir in the hazelnut praline. Whisk in the eggs, one at a time, then stir in the ground hazelnuts, the sifted flour and baking powder and finally the cream.

Transfer the mixture to the loaf tin with the insert in place and pipe a line of butter down the middle of the batter (see page 16). Bake the cake for 1 hour.

When the cake comes out of the oven, leave it to stand in the tin for a few minutes before removing the insert (see page 18). Turn out the cake onto a wire rack and leave it to cool completely before filling it.

To make the praline cream, whip the well-chilled cream with the mascarpone and icing sugar. When the cream is holding its shape, add the praline and whisk again. Spoon about one-third of the cream into a piping bag fitted with a 16 mm (⅔ inch) plain nozzle and use it to fill the cake (see page 18).

Spoon the rest of the cream into a piping bag fitted with a large rope piping nozzle and pipe it on top of the cake. Dust the piped cream with the extra chopped hazelnuts.

OUTSIDE THE BOX

CAPPUCCINO CAKE 165

ARDÈCHE-INSPIRED CHESTNUT CAKE 167

MULLED WINE CAKE 171

ORANGE FLOWER AND PISTACHIO 172

MARSEILLE PASTIS 175

CHRISTMAS IN ROME 176

CASABLANCA TEA 178

CARAMEL POPCORN 181

A TASTE OF THE UNEXPECTED

In this final chapter, I've brought together some more original recipes with unusual ingredient combinations and flavours. A hot drink, an aperitif, a dessert, a snack... several moments of indulgence during the day are represented, with cakes to enjoy all year round. Are you looking for a different sweet cake? One with red wine, for example, or popcorn? What about with tea, pastis or ricotta? With a little imagination, the unexpected and surprising become delicious!

CAPPUCCINO CAKE

 Serves 6–8 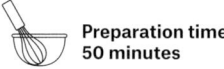 **Preparation time:** 50 minutes   **Cooking time:** 50 minutes

A number of cakes inspired by hot drinks are featured in this book, but cappuccino is particularly suited to the role. To recapture the sensual sweetness of this popular breakfast drink, I've created a cake with the aroma of coffee, a heart of caramel and a cloud-like topping of whipped cream. For this recipe, you will need a loaf tin with a cylinder insert.

CAKE BATTER

- 150 g (5 oz) softened butter, plus extra for greasing the tin and piping
- 180 g (6 oz) plain flour, sifted, plus extra for dusting the tin
- 70 ml (2¾ fl oz) whipping cream
- 18 g (¾ oz) instant coffee granules or powder
- 180 g (6 oz) caster sugar
- 3 eggs
- 2 tablespoons cold espresso
- 7 g (1½ teaspoons) baking powder

COFFEE SOAK

- 25 ml (1 fl oz) made-up espresso coffee
- 2 teaspoons water

continues overleaf >>>

Preheat the oven to 160ºC (325ºF), Gas Mark 3. Butter and flour both your loaf tin and the cylinder insert, and fit the insert into the tin (see page 18).

To make the cake batter, warm the cream, then stir in the instant coffee.

Beat the softened butter with the caster sugar, then whisk in the eggs, one by one. Pour in the espresso, then fold in the sifted flour and baking powder. Finally, stir in the coffee-flavoured cream.

Transfer the batter to the loaf tin and pipe a line of butter down the middle of the batter (see page 16). Bake the cake for 50 minutes.

To make the coffee soak, mix the coffee and water together and brush it over the cake when it comes out of the oven. Leave the cake to cool in the tin before removing the insert and turning it out (see page 18).

CAPPUCCINO CAKE (continued)

COFFEE CARAMEL CREAM FILLING

75 g (3 oz) caster sugar

50 ml (2 fl oz) whipping cream

4 g (1 scant teaspoon) instant coffee granules or powder

25 g (1 oz) butter, diced

MILK CHOCOLATE ICING

250 g (8 oz) milk chocolate with 40% cacao

2 tablespoons plus 1 teaspoon neutral oil, such as grapeseed

CHANTILLY CREAM

100 ml (3½ fl oz) whipping cream

10 g (½ oz) icing sugar

To make the coffee caramel cream filling, prepare a dry caramel by adding the caster sugar a little at a time to a saucepan set over a medium heat until the sugar has melted and becomes a rich amber colour. At the same time, heat the cream with the instant coffee granules in a separate pan, then pour it into the caramel in a thin, steady stream, whisking constantly. When the caramel is smooth, take the pan off the heat and stir in the diced butter. Leave the caramel to cool completely, then spoon it into a piping bag and fill the cake with it (see page 18).

Make the icing following the instructions on page 22. Place the cake on a wire rack and pour the icing over it, spreading it in an even layer. Leave until the icing has set.

For the chantilly cream, whip the cream with the icing sugar. When it is holding its shape, spoon the cream into a piping bag fitted with a plain nozzle and pipe it in small mounds on top of the cake. Store the cake in the refrigerator until ready to serve.

ARDÈCHE-INSPIRED CHESTNUT CAKE

 Serves 6-8

 Preparation time: 50 minutes

 Cooking time: 55 minutes

It's time to head to the Ardèche, which is represented by a cake made with chestnut flour and filled with chestnut ganache. My advice is to use just a little sweet chestnut cream in order to give a more pronounced flavour. For this recipe, you will need a loaf tin with a cylinder insert.

CAKE BATTER

120 g (4 oz) softened butter, plus extra for greasing the tin and piping

70 g (2¾ oz) plain flour, sifted, plus extra for dusting the tin

40 g (1½ oz) caster sugar

1 tablespoon vanilla extract

250 g (8 oz) chestnut cream

4 eggs

20 g (¾ oz) ground almonds

60 g (2¼ oz) chestnut flour

7 g (1½ teaspoons) baking powder

2 tablespoons plus 2 teaspoons whipping cream

VANILLA SOAKING SYRUP

2 tablespoons water

2 teaspoons vanilla extract

25 g (1 oz) caster sugar

continues overleaf >>>

Preheat the oven to 160ºC (325ºF), Gas Mark 3. Butter and flour both your loaf tin and the cylinder insert, and fit the insert into the tin (see page 18).

To make the cake batter, beat the softened butter with the sugar and vanilla, then stir in the chestnut cream. When the batter is evenly mixed, whisk in the eggs, one at a time, then fold in the ground almonds, sifted flour, chestnut flour and baking powder, and finally the cream.

Transfer the batter to the loaf tin and pipe a line of butter down the middle of the batter (see page 16). Bake the cake for 55 minutes.

To make the vanilla soaking syrup, put the 3 ingredients in a saucepan and stir until the mixture comes to the boil and the sugar has dissolved.

When the cake comes out of the oven, brush the syrup over it and leave the cake to cool in the tin before removing the insert (see page 18) and turning out the cake onto a wire rack.

ARDÈCHE-INSPIRED CHESTNUT CAKE (continued)

CHOCOLATE AND CHESTNUT CREAM GANACHE

40 g (1½ oz) dark chocolate with 66% cacao, chopped

90 g (3¼ oz) chestnut cream

3 tablespoons whipping cream

2 teaspoons honey

10 g (½ oz) butter, diced

DARK CHOCOLATE ICING

250 g (8 oz) dark chocolate with 66% cacao

3 tablespoons neutral oil, such as grapeseed

To make the ganache, melt the chocolate in a bain-marie, then add the chestnut cream. At the same time, bring the cream and honey to the boil in a separate saucepan. Add the cream mixture to the chocolate in 3 equal quantities, stirring well between each addition. Finally, add the diced butter and whisk the ganache with a hand blender until it is smooth and creamy.

Spoon the ganache into a piping bag. When the cake is completely cold, fill it with the ganache (see page 18).

Prepare the icing following the instructions on page 22. Pour the icing over the cake and leave until the icing has set. Keep the cake refrigerated until ready to serve.

MULLED WINE CAKE

 **Serves** 6–8

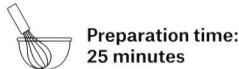 **Preparation time:** 25 minutes

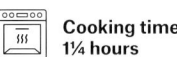 **Cooking time:** 1¼ hours

The inspiration for this mulled wine-style cake is an Alsatian cake called *rotweinkuchen*, which is made with red wine and spices. It's a cake to enjoy in the middle of winter for a truly indulgent evening.

CAKE BATTER

180 g (6 oz) softened butter, plus extra for greasing the tin and piping

190 g (6½ oz) plain flour, sifted, plus extra for dusting the tin

90 g (3¼ oz) caster sugar

220 g (7½ oz) eggs (about 4 eggs)

½ vanilla pod, split lengthways and seeds scraped out

2 tablespoons ground cinnamon

2¼ teaspoons unsweetened cocoa powder

7 g (1½ teaspoons) baking powder

200 ml (7 fl oz) red wine (I use Chianti)

130 g (4¼ oz) dark chocolate

Preheat the oven to 160°C (325°F), Gas Mark 3. Butter and flour your loaf tin.

Beat the softened butter with the sugar, then whisk in the eggs, one at a time. Add the vanilla seeds, cinnamon and cocoa, followed by the sifted flour and baking powder.

Stir in the red wine a little at a time.

Chop the chocolate finely and mix it into the batter.

Transfer the batter to the loaf tin and pipe a line of butter down the middle of the batter (see page 16). Bake the cake for 1¼ hours.

When the cake comes out of the oven, leave it to cool in the tin for a few minutes before turning it out onto a wire rack. Leave it to cool completely before eating.

ORANGE FLOWER AND PISTACHIO

 Serves 6-8

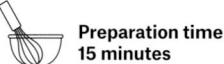 **Preparation time:** 15 minutes

 **Cooking time:** 1 hour

Two ingredients used together with increasing frequency in cake making are orange flower water and pistachios. Add a little olive oil for a subtle touch and a uniquely moist texture, and you have a cake that will take your taste buds on a journey to distant shores.

CAKE BATTER

- a little butter for greasing the tin and piping
- 175 g (6 oz) plain flour, sifted, plus extra for dusting the tin
- 3 eggs
- 180 g (6¼ oz) caster sugar
- 60 g (2¼ oz) Pistachio Butter (see page 28)
- 85 ml (3¼ fl oz) olive oil
- 2 teaspoons orange flower water
- 6 g (1¼ teaspoons) baking powder
- 75 ml (3 fl oz) whipping cream

Preheat the oven to 160ºC (325ºF), Gas Mark 3. Butter and flour your loaf tin.

Whisk the eggs with the sugar until thickened and fluffy, then add the pistachio butter, olive oil and orange flower water. Mix until all the ingredients are evenly combined before folding in the sifted flour and baking powder. Finally, stir in the cream.

Spoon the batter into the loaf tin and pipe a line of butter down the middle of the batter (see page 16). Bake the cake for 1 hour.

When the cake comes out of the oven, turn it out onto a wire rack and leave it to cool.

MARSEILLE PASTIS

 Serves 6–8  **Preparation time:** 10 minutes   **Cooking time:** 55 minutes

A nod to my home city of Marseille, where pastis is known as *le petit jaune* ('the little yellow one'). This cake will please all fans of the refreshing aniseed drink from Provence.

CAKE BATTER

120 g (4 oz) softened butter, plus extra for greasing the tin and piping

200 g (7 oz) plain flour, sifted, plus extra for dusting the tin

140 g (4½ oz) caster sugar

3 eggs

50 ml (2 fl oz) pastis (I use Ricard)

6 g (1¼ teaspoons) baking powder

50 ml (2 fl oz) whipping cream

Preheat the oven to 160ºC (325ºF), Gas Mark 3. Butter and flour your loaf tin.

Beat the softened butter with the caster sugar, then add the eggs, whisking them in one by one.

Stir in the pastis, then fold in the sifted flour and baking powder.

Finally, stir in the cream.

Transfer the batter to the loaf tin and pipe a line of butter down the middle of the batter (see page 16). Bake the cake for 55 minutes.

When the cake comes out of the oven, leave it to cool in the tin for a few minutes before turning it out onto a wire rack to cool completely.

CHRISTMAS IN ROME

 Serves 6-8

 **Preparation time:** 10 minutes

 Cooking time: 55 minutes

With notes of cinnamon, chocolate and citrus fruits, we are immediately transported to Christmastime, but not just anywhere. In this recipe, the butter is replaced by ricotta and the fresh Italian cheese brings a special texture to the cake.

CAKE BATTER

| a little butter for greasing the tin and piping |
| 200 g (7 oz) plain flour, sifted, plus extra for dusting the tin |
| 160 g (5½ oz) cow's milk ricotta |
| finely grated zest of 1 orange |
| finely grated zest of 1 lemon |
| 4 g (1 scant teaspoon) ground cinnamon |
| 110 g (3¾ oz) caster sugar |
| 3 eggs |
| 6 g (1¼ teaspoons) baking powder |
| 3 tablespoons whipping cream |
| 35 g (1¼ oz) dark chocolate with 66% cacao, chopped |

Preheat the oven to 160°C (325°F), Gas Mark 3. Butter and flour your loaf tin.

Mix the ricotta with the citrus zests and the cinnamon. Add the sugar, then whisk in the eggs, one at a time. Fold in the sifted flour and baking powder, followed by the cream and finally the chopped chocolate.

Spoon the batter into the loaf tin and pipe a line of butter down the middle of the batter (see page 16). Bake the cake for 55 minutes.

When the cake comes out of the oven, turn it out onto a wire rack and leave to cool.

CASABLANCA TEA

 Serves 6-8 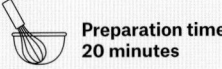 **Preparation time:** 20 minutes   **Cooking time:** 55 minutes

What could be better than a cake with the fragrance of an aromatic tea to accompany your afternoon cup of tea? For this recipe, I've used Casablanca tea from the French gourmet tea company Mariage Frères, but you can choose whatever one you wish, as long as you vary the brewing time to suit your chosen tea.

CAKE BATTER

50 g (2 oz) butter, plus extra for greasing the tin and piping

200 g (7 oz) plain flour, sifted, plus extra for dusting the tin

3 eggs

180 g (6 oz) caster sugar

60 ml (2¼ fl oz) black tea of your choice, cooled

6 g (1¼ teaspoons) baking powder

50 ml (2 fl oz) whipping cream

1 teaspoon tea leaves of choice

TEA SOAK

2 tablespoons hot black tea of choice

FOR DECORATION

multi-coloured edible dried petals (often sold in tea bags for brewing)

Preheat the oven to 160°C (325°F), Gas Mark 3. Butter and flour your loaf tin.

Melt the butter and leave it to cool to lukewarm.

Whisk the eggs with the sugar until thickened and fluffy, then whisk in the cold tea. Fold in the sifted flour and baking powder, followed by the lukewarm butter and the whipping cream. Finally, stir in the tea leaves.

Transfer the batter to the loaf tin and pipe a line of butter down the middle of the batter (see page 16). Bake the cake for 55 minutes.

When the cake comes out of the oven, brush it immediately with the tea soak. Leave the cake in the tin until it is completely cold before turning it out.

Decorate with multi-coloured edible dried petals sprinkled on top.

CARAMEL POPCORN

 **Serves** 6–8　　 **Preparation time:** 35 minutes　　 **Cooking time:** 1 hour

Pick a great film, cut yourself a slice of cake, close your eyes and you are at the cinema! When I was developing the recipe for this cake, on one attempt I forgot to add the sugar – funnily enough, I was pleasantly surprised by the result. So, if you prefer salty popcorn, do as I did and you'll have the ideal cake to enjoy with an aperitif.

CAKE BATTER

50 g (2 oz) softened butter, plus extra for greasing the tin and piping

180 g (6 oz) plain flour, sifted, plus extra for dusting the tin

250 ml (8 fl oz) whipping cream

75 g (3 oz) caramelized popcorn

75 g (3 oz) plain popcorn

140 g (4½ oz) caster sugar

3 eggs

6 g (1¼ teaspoons) baking powder

2 tablespoons full-fat milk

FOR DECORATION

75 g (3 oz) white chocolate, chopped

50 g (2 oz) popcorn (this can be a mixture of caramelized popcorn and plain or salty popcorn, as you wish)

Preheat the oven to 160ºC (325ºF), Gas Mark 3. Butter and flour your loaf tin.

To make the cake batter, heat the cream, then stir in both popcorns. Leave them to melt for a few minutes, then blend the mixture lightly in a food processor, so some pieces of popcorn remain.

Beat the softened butter with the sugar in a mixing bowl, then beat in the eggs, one at a time.

Add the popcorn cream to the mixture, followed by the sifted flour and baking powder. Finally, add the milk and mix well.

Transfer the batter to the loaf tin and pipe a line of butter down the middle of the batter (see page 16). Bake the cake for 1 hour.

When the cake comes out of the oven, leave it to cool in the tin for a few minutes before turning it out onto a wire rack.

When the cake is completely cold, gently melt the white chocolate without letting the temperature of it rise above 35ºC (95ºF). Spread the melted chocolate all over the top of the cake and press the popcorn into it before it sets.

GLOSSARY

UK	US
caster sugar	superfine sugar
clingfilm	plastic wrap
cocoa powder	unsweetened chocolate powder
cornflour	cornstarch
cream:	
double or whipping cream	heavy cream
single or pouring cream	light cream
desiccated coconut	unsweetened shredded coconut
full-fat milk	whole milk
grated	shredded
hazelnut	filbert
icing	frosting
icing sugar	confectioners' sugar
loaf tin	loaf pan
muslin	cheesecloth
natural yogurt	plain yogurt
plain flour	all-purpose flour
vanilla pod	vanilla bean

INDEX

A

almonds
  banana, chocolate and peanut cake 138
  blonde chocolate and almond icing 102, 136
  creamy cheesecake loaf 18, 149
  dark chocolate and almond icing 136
  gluten-free amaretto and almond liqueur 102
  perfectly spiced carrot cake 141
amaretto liqueur
  gluten-free amaretto and almond liqueur 102
apples
  Normandy apple and caramel 130–1
  seasonal fruits your way 136
Ardèche-inspired chestnut cake 167
Aztec hot chocolate 58

B

banana, chocolate and peanut cake 138
basil
  refreshing lime and basil 111
berry fruits
  seasonal fruits your way 136
blonde chocolate
  blonde chocolate and almond icing 102, 136
  blonde chocolate icing 26, 60
  blonde chocolate and nut icing 26
  triple chocolate marble 79
blood orange cake 112
brownies
  the ultimate chocolate brownie 63
butter
  piping on top of cakes 16

C

candied orange peel
  festive chocolate orange cake 122
cappuccino cake 165
caramel
  caramel popcorn 181
  crème brûlée 150–1
  Normandy apple and caramel 130–1
  peanut and caramel 105
  salted caramel 42
carrots
  perfectly spiced carrot cake 141
Casablanca tea 178
cheesecake loaf, creamy 149
chestnut cream
  Ardèche-inspired chestnut cake 167
chocolate
  Ardèche-inspired chestnut cake 167
  Aztec hot chocolate 58
  banana, chocolate and peanut cake 138
  blonde chocolate and almond icing 102, 136
  blonde chocolate icing 26
  blonde chocolate and nut icing 26
  cappuccino cake 165
  caramel popcorn 181
  chocolate chip cookie cake 152
  chocolate and coconut cake 132
  chocolate fondant 57
  chocolate icing 22
  chocolate and pistachio marble 71
  Christmas in Rome 176
  classic marble cake 71
  cozy cinnamon marble 83–4
  dark chocolate and almond icing 136
  dark chocolate icing 24
  dark chocolate and nut icing 24
  festive chocolate orange cake 122
  giant madeleine 157
  hazelnut coffee cake 96
  hazelnut financier 154
  hazelnut gianduja 51–2
  the hazelnut lover's cake 92
  irresistible marshmallow 53–4
  matcha marble 86
  milk chocolate and hazelnut icing 92
  milk chocolate icing 25, 105, 136
  milk chocolate and nut icing 25
  mocha 60
  mogador marble 80–2
  mulled wine cake 171
  nostalgic chocolate and hazelnut spread cake 64
  triple chocolate marble 79
  the ultimate chocolate brownie 63
Christmas in Rome 176
cinnamon

Christmas in Rome 176
cozy cinnamon marble
   83–4
mulled wine cake 171
perfectly spiced carrot
   cake 141
citrus fruits 106–25
   blood orange cake 112
   citrus fruit medley 125
   deliciously tangy lime and
      lemon cream 121
   festive chocolate orange
      cake 122
   lemon meringue cake
      114–15
   mojito cake 118
   refreshing lime and basil
      cream 111
classic French yogurt cake 34
classic marble cake 71
clementines
   citrus fruit medley 125
cloud cake 38
cocoa powder
   banana, chocolate and
      peanut cake 138
   chocolate and pistachio
      marble 71
   classic marble cake 71
   cozy cinnamon marble
      83–4
   festive chocolate orange
      cake 122
   mulled wine cake 171
   peanut and caramel 105
   tiramisu cake 18, 146
   ultimate hazelnut ganache
      74–5
coconut
   chocolate and coconut
      cake 132

coffee
   cappuccino cake 165
   hazelnut coffee cake 96
   mocha 60
   tiramisu cake 18, 146
   cozy cinnamon marble 83–4
cream
   Ardèche-inspired chestnut
      cake 167
   Aztec hot chocolate 58
   blood orange cake 112
   cappuccino cake 165
   caramel popcorn 181
   Casablanca tea 178
   chocolate and pistachio
      marble 71
   Christmas in Rome 176
   citrus fruit medley 125
   classic marble cake 71
   cozy cinnamon marble
      83–4
   creamy cheesecake loaf
      18, 149
   crème brûlée 150–1
   deliciously tangy lime and
      lemon 121
   festive chocolate orange
      cake 122
   hazelnut coffee cake 96
   the hazelnut lover's cake 92
   honey nut breakfast cake 98
   irresistible marshmallow
      53–4
   lemon meringue cake
      114–15
   Marseille pastis 175
   matcha marble 86
   mogador marble 80–2
   mojito cake 118
   Normandy apple and
      caramel 130–1

   nostalgic chocolate and
      hazelnut spread cake 64
   orange flower and
      pistachio 172
   Paris-Brest cake 18, 158
   peanut and caramel 105
   pecan vanilla 101
   refreshing lime and basil 111
   rum and vanilla 41
   salted caramel 42
   Sicilian pistachio 95
   Speculoos special 45
   tiramisu cake 18, 146
   ultimate hazelnut ganache
      74–5
cream cheese
   creamy cheesecake loaf
      18, 149
   perfectly spiced carrot
      cake 141
   pumpkin spice 135
crème brûlée 150–1
cylinder inserts
   filling the cavity 18

D

dark chocolate
   Ardèche-inspired chestnut
      cake 167
   Aztec hot chocolate 58
   banana, chocolate and
      peanut cake 138
   chocolate chip cookie
      cake 152
   chocolate fondant 57
   Christmas in Rome 176
   dark chocolate and almond
      icing 136
   dark chocolate icing 24, 133
   dark chocolate and nut
      icing 24

festive chocolate orange
    cake 122
giant madeleine 157
hazelnut financier 154
mocha 60
mulled wine cake 171
triple chocolate marble 79
the ultimate chocolate
    brownie 63

E

edible dried petals
    Casablanca tea 178

F

festive chocolate orange
    cake 122
feuilletines
    ultimate hazelnut ganache
        74–5
fondant, chocolate 57
fruit
    marbled summer fruits
        76
    seasonal fruits your way
        136

G

gianduja
    hazelnut gianduja 51–2
giant madeleine 157
gingerbread spice mix
    Aztec hot chocolate 58
Grand Marnier
    blood orange cake 112
grapefruit
    citrus fruit medley 125
Greek yogurt
    creamy cheesecake loaf
        18, 149

H

hazelnut butter
    hazelnut coffee cake 96
    the hazelnut lover's cake 92
    lemon meringue cake
        114–15
    ultimate hazelnut ganache
        74–5
hazelnut praline 27
    Paris-Brest cake 18, 158
    ultimate hazelnut ganache
        74–5
hazelnut spread
    nostalgic chocolate and
        hazelnut spread cake 64
hazelnuts
    chocolate chip cookie
        cake 152
    cozy cinnamon marble
        83–4
    hazelnut coffee cake 96
    hazelnut financier 154
    hazelnut gianduja 51–2
    the hazelnut lover's cake
        92
    hazelnut praline 27
    lemon meringue cake
        114–15
    milk chocolate and
        hazelnut icing 92
    nostalgic chocolate and
        hazelnut spread cake 64
    Paris-Brest cake 18, 158
    perfectly spiced carrot
        cake 141
    ultimate hazelnut ganache
        74–5
honey
    Ardèche-inspired chestnut
        cake 167
    hazelnut coffee cake 96

honey nut breakfast cake
    98
ultimate hazelnut ganache
    74–5

I

icing
    blonde chocolate and
        almond icing 102, 136
    blonde chocolate icing 26
    blonde chocolate and nut
        icing 26
    blood orange cake 112
    chocolate icing 22
    dark chocolate and
        almond icing 136
    dark chocolate icing 24,
        122
    dark chocolate and nut
        icing 24
    festive chocolate orange
        cake 122
    giant madeleine 157
    milk chocolate and
        hazelnut icing 92
    milk chocolate icing
        25, 105
    seasonal fruits your way
        136
Italian meringue
    lemon meringue cake
        114–15

K

kumquats
    citrus fruit medley 125

L

lemons
    Christmas in Rome 176
    citrus fruit medley 125

deliciously tangy lime and lemon cream 121
lemon meringue cake 114–15
limes
  citrus fruit medley 125
  deliciously tangy lime and lemon 121
  marbled summer fruits 76
  mojito cake 118
  refreshing lime and basil 111

M
madeleine, giant 157
marbled cakes
  chocolate and pistachio marble 71
  classic marble cake 71
  cozy cinnamon marble 83–4
  marbled summer fruits 76
  matcha marble 86
  mogador marble 80–2
  technique for making 16
  triple chocolate marble 79
  ultimate hazelnut ganache 74–5
marbled summer fruits 76
Marseille pastis 175
marshmallow, irresistible 53–4
mascarpone
  Normandy apple and caramel 130–1
  Paris-Brest cake 18, 158
  tiramisu cake 18, 146
matcha marble 86
meringue
  lemon meringue cake 114–15

milk chocolate
  cappuccino cake 165
  chocolate and coconut cake 132
  cozy cinnamon marble 83–4
  hazelnut coffee cake 96
  hazelnut gianduja 51–2
  the hazelnut lover's cake 92
  milk chocolate icing 25, 105
  mogador marble 80–2
  triple chocolate marble 79
mint
  mojito cake 118
mocha 60
mogador marble 80–2
mojito cake 118
mulled wine cake 171
muscovado sugar
  vanilla and muscovado 37

N
Normandy apple and caramel 130–1
nostalgic chocolate and hazelnut spread cake 64
nuts
  banana, chocolate and peanut cake 138
  blonde chocolate and almond icing 102, 136
  blonde chocolate and nut icing 26
  chocolate chip cookie cake 152
  chocolate and pistachio marble 71
  creamy cheesecake loaf 18, 149

  dark chocolate and almond icing 136
  dark chocolate and nut icing 24
  gluten-free amaretto and almond liqueur 102
  hazelnut coffee cake 96
  the hazelnut lover's cake 92
  honey nut breakfast cake 98
  lemon meringue cake 114–15
  milk chocolate and nut icing 25
  nut butters 28
  orange flower and pistachio 172
  Paris-Brest cake 18, 158
  peanut and caramel 105
  pecan vanilla 101
  perfectly spiced carrot cake 141
  Sicilian pistachio 95
  ultimate hazelnut ganache 74–5

O
orange flower and pistachio 172
oranges
  blood orange cake 112
  Christmas in Rome 176
  festive chocolate orange cake 122
  giant madeleine 157

P
Paris-Brest cake 18, 158
passion fruit
  mogador marble 80–2
  seasonal fruits your way 136

pastis
   Marseille pastis 175
peanut butter
   banana, chocolate and peanut cake 138
   peanut and caramel 105
peanuts
   peanut and caramel 105
pears
   seasonal fruits your way 136
pecan nuts
   pecan vanilla 101
   perfectly spiced carrot cake 141
pine nuts
   honey nut breakfast cake 98
pistachio butter
   chocolate and pistachio marble 71
   orange flower and pistachio 172
   Sicilian pistachio 95
pistachios
   Sicilian pistachio 95
popcorn
   caramel popcorn 181
praline, hazelnut 27
   ultimate hazelnut ganache 74–5
pumpkin spice 135

Q
quatre épices spice mix
   Aztec hot chocolate 58

R
raspberries
   marbled summer fruits 76
   matcha marble 86
   seasonal fruits your way 136

red wine
   mulled wine cake 171
ricotta
   Christmas in Rome 176
rum
   mojito cake 118
   rum and vanilla 41

S
salted caramel 42
Speculoos special 45
spices
   perfectly spiced carrot cake 141
   pumpkin spice 135
storing cakes 18

T
tea
   Casablanca tea 178
tiramisu cake 18, 146
tonka beans
   the ultimate chocolate brownie 63
triple chocolate marble 79

U
ultimate hazelnut ganache 74–5

V
vanilla
   Ardèche-inspired chestnut cake 167
   chocolate chip cookie cake 152
   classic marble cake 71
   cloud cake 38
   crème brûlée 150–1
   hazelnut financier 154

irresistible marshmallow 53–4
mulled wine cake 171
Normandy apple and caramel 130–1
pecan vanilla 101
perfectly spiced carrot cake 141
pumpkin spice 135
rum and vanilla 41
vanilla and muscovado 37

W
walnuts
   perfectly spiced carrot cake 141
white chocolate
   caramel popcorn 181
   matcha marble 86
   triple chocolate marble 79
wine
   mulled wine cake 171

Y
yogurt
   classic French yogurt cake 34
   creamy cheesecake loaf 18, 149

ACKNOWLEDGEMENTS

First of all, my thanks go to all my followers and readers of my blog, without whom this great adventure and this book would never have existed.

Thank you also to all my family for their support and to my taste testers who will recognize themselves. Many of them forgot about their diets to help me improve the recipes in this book.

Finally, thank you to Sandrine for her wonderful photographs that so beautifully illustrate all the cakes and to Jeanne and the team at Hachette for trusting and supporting me during the entire project.

ABOUT THE AUTHOR

Flavie Millet-Joannon is the creator of the blog and Instagram account @iletaitungâteau, where she shares her recipes and top baking tips with her community of over 130,000 followers. Her passion for baking led her to obtain the Certificat d'Aptitude Professionnelle, a national French qualification for bakers and pastry chefs.